The
Step-By-Step
Wedding
Planner

Your Guide to the Perfect Wedding Day

Eve Anderson

The
Step-By-Step
Wedding
Planner

Eve Anderson

foulsham

LONDON · NEW YORK · TORONTO · SYDNEY

foulsham

Bennetts Close, Cippenham, Berkshire, SL1 5AP

Other titles in this series:

The Best Man's Organiser
The Wedding Gift Organiser
The Wedding Organiser
Wedding Speeches and Jokes
Wedding Etiquette

Disclaimer

While every effort has been made to ensure the accuracy of all the information contained within this book, neither the author nor the publisher can be liable for any errors. In particular, since laws change from time to time, it is vital that each individual should check relevant legal details for themselves.

ISBN 0–572–01589–5

Copyright © 1990 W. Foulsham & Co. Ltd

Reprinted 1995, 1998

Printed in England by Redwood Books, Trowbridge, Wiltshire

Contents

Foreword

CONGRATULATIONS! You are engaged and are planning your wedding day. The next few months will be a busy and exciting time for you. There are so many things to think about, so many details to plan and decisions to make. You may be booking churches and hotels, buying dresses and shoes, interviewing caterers and choosing menus, selecting cars – and all the time keeping your head, and keeping everyone happy!

Sound complicated and a bit daunting? Well, no one would deny that there will be plenty to keep you busy, but if you plan carefully, keep a note of all the details, and sift and select the advice you are given, it will all go smoothly.

The Step-by-Step Wedding Planner will help you to plan a wonderful wedding day. It is based not just on etiquette, but on the experiences of brides who really know what it is like to plan a wedding, and who want your wedding day to be as perfect as their own.

Read through the book carefully, and you will find information on every aspect of wedding planning. We have tried to include all the information you will need, but if you are planning something very unusual, you can easily adjust the information to suit your needs.

The second section of the book consists of a series of checklists for easy reference so that you can use the book as a complete planner for your special day. You can keep all those vital telephone numbers handy, tick off the jobs you have done, and remind yourself what remains to be done. Fill in and personalise the lists as you go along, so nothing is forgotten.

Start planning well in advance and set your budget early. Then you can take your time and enjoy planning your wedding, and make sure that your wedding day is perfect.

Introduction

FOR MOST couples, their wedding day marks the start of their new life together. The ceremony and celebrations provide both a public announcement and a private commitment, something to be remembered for the rest of their lives. It is an exciting and perhaps daunting prospect. If you have been involved in the arrangements for a sister's or brother's wedding you may already have lots of ideas. But many couples will be starting from scratch. How much services and supplies will cost, where you obtain them and how far in advance you need to book them are all a mystery. One thing is certain; you want a wonderful day to mark the start of your married life. So what kind of wedding will you choose? How much will it cost? And where will you find out how to go about planning that very special day? The answer is, here in *The Step-by-Step Wedding Planner*.

This book is designed to give you as much information as possible about as many options as possible so that you can make an informed decision on the kind of wedding you will have. Once you have done that, there is a wealth of practical information on how to go about organising the day, and checklists at each stage to help ensure that nothing is forgotten. But the book includes not only the etiquette and basic information, we also try to tell you what to expect on the day and in your future lives, both practically and emotionally. Our aim is to help you avoid as many problems as possible.

The chapters deal with all aspects of wedding planning. We try to give some ideas of what to look for in making your decisions, and suggest some questions to ask before making your final choice. Although no book can cover every situation, we have tried to give you specific examples as well as to cover the general. Our hope is that even if we have not included answers to every one of your questions, by reading this book you will gain enough information to know where to find the answers you need.

There are lots of things to think about, and some will be mentioned in several chapters; so the first thing to do is to read through the whole book. Keep a pen or pencil handy, and jot down any comments, queries or ideas you may have as you go along, listing them under headings such as seating plan, photographs, food and so on. With luck you will find any questions raised are answered later on in the book; but if not, you will have a record of the things you still want to check and some pointers as to who will be able to help you.

In some areas, such as the catering for the reception for example, you may want expert advice. Don't be afraid to ask the professionals for help and recommendations. They will have handled many similar celebrations and be aware of what is available and how you can make economies.

Setting the budget for your wedding at an early stage is extremely important. Weddings can be very expensive occasions, if you allow them to be. If you have a fixed budget and work within it, then you automatically have a sense of priorities where expenses are concerned, and will be able to choose how you wish to spend your money. After all, it is not how much is spent, but how it is spent which is important.

Traditionally, the cost of a wedding is borne chiefly by the bride's father, but it is a long time since this custom was established, and it is not always relevant today. A wedding can be very expensive, and it is rather unreasonable to expect the bride's father to foot the entire bill if both bride and groom, as well as the groom's parents, are all working.

So these days, the cost of most weddings is split between the bride's and groom's parents, and the couple themselves. Sometimes, the bride's parents pay for most of the wedding, with the bride and groom and the groom's parents opting to pay for specific things, such as the clothes or the drinks at the reception. You may also have a generous relation who would like to pay for something or contribute in one way or another. An aunt might bake and ice the cake, for example, or an uncle might bring a case of champagne.

If your parents and prospective in-laws do not know each other well, they may be embarrassed to talk about the costs, but it is important that everyone knows where they stand, so get them together early on and try to get the conversation going, perhaps over a glass of sherry.

Where etiquette is concerned, it is up to you how much you decide to conform. We have included the relevant information, but weddings are more flexible now than they were in the past, so weigh the information and choose how you want the day to be organised. Don't be ruled by convention. If you don't want a veil, don't have one; if you would rather have a garden party than a formal meal, then that is right for you (but remember the weather, just in case!). The important thing is that the day is arranged how you want it, and that your guests are made to feel welcome and able to enjoy themselves.

You may find that your ideas do not fit exactly with those of your parents, and you feel torn between choosing exactly what you want and following the traditions your families expect you to follow. There are no easy solutions to this, except to listen tactfully, talk about what you all want, and compromise. If your mother had always dreamed of seeing you married in a white lace dress, try to put yourself in her shoes before you suggest a scarlet suit! It is an emotional time for everyone, and a little forethought and understanding will go a long way to making the arrangements easier. You may also receive well-meaning advice from all sides. Don't just switch off; listen diplomatically and pick out any ideas which suit you.

Now to the actual planning. However much time you have, use it all. Start early, and you will have plenty of time to make the right decisions. Leave it too late, and your chosen suppliers may already be booked, forcing you into rushed decisions which may not be the best ones. Work out your timetable based on the checklists at the back of the book, then give yourself a little 'looking-around' time. Read magazines, jot down ideas or keep pictures of dresses, food ideas or flowers you particularly like before you start committing yourself. That way the style of the wedding will emerge in your mind and it will be easier when you come to make final choices.

You and the groom will want to make all the important decisions yourselves, so make sure you talk to him about the plans. This sounds obvious, but is easy to forget! He will have his own opinion, even though he may not be as interested in the details as you are.

Make sure you know what is going on at every stage. Keep this book to hand and record everything in it – names, addresses, telephone numbers, plans, dates. Then you will never need to scrabble for the old envelope on which you wrote down the name of the photographer. Have back-up services jotted down too, just in case, then a quick phone call will sort out what could be have been a problem.

Make the major decisions yourself. Brides who had everything done for them said later that they did not feel it was their wedding. But don't be greedy! The groom, your parents, the groom's parents, your chief bridesmaid, all have roles to play and there is plenty for everyone to do. You will wear yourself out and not enjoy the planning if you try to do too much yourself.

About half way through the planning, you may find that you become fed up with the very thought of weddings. Don't worry; just close the book for a few days and refuse to talk about weddings. Go out for a meal or take a weekend break, then come back to it all fresh – the magic will be there waiting for you.

Your relationship with your future spouse may take a few nose-dives during the planning, too. After all, it is probably the first time you have planned a major event together, and the excitement is bound to affect how you get on with each other. Communication is usually the answer. It does not help to snap at him if things aren't going as well as you hoped. Ask his advice, enlist his support; you'll get on better that way.

The Step-by-Step Wedding Planner is designed to help you prepare for every aspect of your wedding day. But remember to find time to think about what will happen after the wedding. Whatever the scale of your wedding, you are the centre of attention, and you may find that after the excitement is over there is a feeling of anticlimax. This is only natural after all the anticipation and the excitement of the day itself. Try to prepare yourself for this by thinking about the commitment you are making, so you enter marriage seriously and with a determination to make it work.

1 The Engagement and Preparations

The Tradition of Marriage

*J*oining couples in marriage is a tradition which dates back thousands of years, and is a custom which is immersed in ritualistic significance. Nowadays, not much attention is paid to traditions, and it is often difficult to establish why things are done in a particular way. However, we do know that the origins of many of the customs which survive today were originally introduced not merely for enjoyment or convenience, but for a specific purpose usually associated with warding off evil and bringing good luck, prosperity and children to the newly-married couple. Here are some old traditions concerning marriage in general which are perhaps interesting and amusing.

Originally, 'marriage' was often more like kidnap in that a man would seize his chosen woman from her family and carry her off to keep house and bear his children. It did not make a lot of difference whether she was willing or not!

A wife was considered to be a valuable asset as she would cook, clean and bring up a family. Fathers began to appreciate these valuable skills and consequently became more protective towards their unmarried daughters. Prospective husbands then had to prove that they could be good providers and began to offer valuable gifts to the family, or to work off the price of the daughter's hand in marriage. The most famous example of this is Jacob in the Bible who worked for seven years in order to marry Rachael. Rather than marry off his youngest daughter first, her father substituted Rachael for her older sister Leah, and Jacob had to work a further seven years in order to marry his chosen bride.

Later in history, fathers began to offer a dowry to their daughter's husband. This was an insurance against divorce, as the woman now brought something of her own into the marriage and the husband could only control the dowry as long as they stayed married.

In some societies, children were engaged to one another when they were very young. Contracts were drawn up detailing all the arrangements, and these were considered legally binding. If one family backed out of the arrangements, they could forfeit half their property!

'Engagements' really began in the sixth century when King Ethelbert deemed it illegal for a man to 'steal' the woman of his choice from her family, thereby protecting fathers from losing 'valuable assets'. The penalty for stealing a woman was a fine of eighty shillings to compensate for lost 'manpower'.

The 'wedding', as it was known, sealed an agreement between the groom and the bride's father that a marriage would take place.

Although engagements no longer have any legal significance, they are still viewed as a serious commitment and a public announcement of a couple's final decision and their intention to share the rest of their lives together. A couple's decision to marry usually emerges from the mutual understanding of their relationship. The engagement period allows the couple an opportunity to consider and discuss their future life and prospects regarding finances, work, sex and children. These days a proposal of marriage could easily come from the woman as from the man but usually, when the woman has replied affirmatively to the all important question "Will you marry me?", *she* then has the right to name the day.

Announcements

Informal

Announcing an engagement is much less formal today but it is still worth bearing in mind a few pointers!

Although these days it is the exception rather than the rule, taking the trouble to ask the girl's father is still one of the best ways of establishing an amicable son-in-law/father-in-law relationship. Parents are naturally deeply concerned about the future happiness of their offspring and a quiet discussion with them before the news goes public should relieve any anxieties. It is important to ensure that there are no absolute objections to the marriage and that the bride's parents are satisfied that their prospective son-in-law can provide the happiness and support the daughter is expecting.

Both sets of parents should be informed as soon as possible and should be the first outsiders to hear the news. It is traditional for the bride's parents to be the first to learn of the news and this is only common courtesy if they are expected to pay all or part of the wedding costs. Face-to-face communication is always desirable but if this is impossible, a telephone call is the next best option.

It is only natural that when a couple become engaged, they want to tell "the world", and of course family and friends want to share the news and convey their best wishes. However, the announcement should not be made at someone else's wedding!

Most couples like to inform close relatives and friends personally or by telephone, and many write to other relations and friends announcing their engagement and giving a few details about their fiancé and future plans. If communicating by post, it is advisable to post all letters at the same time so that no one feels excluded from the news. A tick list naming all those to be informed, such as the one overleaf, is a good way of keeping track of progress.

If both sets of parents are unacquainted, arrangements should be made for them to meet and socialise at a family dinner, perhaps, which is usually given (paid for) by the groom's parents if the bride's parents will be paying the major contribution to the cost of the wedding.

11

Informal Announcements							
Name	Personal Visit ✔	Letter ✔	Address	Done ✔	Tel. Call ✔	Telephone Number	Done ✔

Formal

Some couples choose to announce their engagement officially and as a surprise at a party given by the bride's parents who, along with the groom's parents, should already know the news. The bride's father makes the official announcement at the celebration and the bride's mother issues the invitations. The chart overleaf may be useful to ensure that no one is forgotten. Other couples prefer a party purely for friends when they themselves make the announcement.

Usually if there is to be a formal official engagement, the engagement ring is not worn in public until the engagement has been officially announced.

Following the announcement, it is customary for both sets of parents to share some time together. If this is impossible because of long distance, it is a thoughtful gesture if they exchange letters mentioning their happiness at the news and that they are looking forward to meeting one another at the wedding.

Some couples choose to announce their engagement in the national newspapers, but for most, an announcement in their local paper is a satisfactory way of informing casual friends and neighbours of their engagement. The parents (usually the mother) of the bride-to-be, or the bride herself, assumes responsibility for sending the announcement to the editor of the chosen newspaper, whether national or local, a week or so beforehand, stating the date on which the announcement is to appear and including a daytime telephone number in case of queries. Many papers have a standard form for obtaining this information. Whether writing out the announcement or filling in a form, the script must be clearly legible with all text spelled correctly. A point to bear in mind is that if a full address is included in the announcement, then many circulars from advertisers of wedding services may follow!

Example copy:

Formal

> Mr S South and
> Miss/Ms N North
>
> The engagement is announced between
> Sam
> only son of
> Mr and Mrs Sid South of Southton
> and
> Nel
> youngest daughter of
> Mr and Mrs Ned North of Northton

OR

> A marriage has been arranged
> (and will shortly take place)
> between
> Mr Sam South
> son of . . .
> of . . .
> and
> Nel
> daughter of . . .
> of . . .

OR

> Mr and Mrs Ned North
> are pleased to announce
> the engagement of
> their daughter
> Nel
> to
> Mr Sam South
> son of Mrs and Mrs . . .
> of . . .

Less Formal

> Nel and Nancy North
> are delighted to announce
> the engagement of their daughter
> Nel
> to
> Sam
> son of . . .

Formal Announcements		
Name	**Address**	**Done** ✔

On a more humorous note, on country farms where bees are kept, it is customary to tell the bees of the forthcoming marriage and to give them some of the wedding cake!

Well Wishers

Well wishers should congratulate only the groom — women are not to be congratulated but wished every future happiness.

Engagement Ring

Although commonplace, there is no necessity for the bride-to-be to have or to wear an engagement ring but if desired, its design can take any form — it does not have to be a diamond. Birthstones (or Month stones) which are associated with particular months and symbolise specific personal qualities are a popular choice and are said to be luck-bringers in engagement rings. A list of their symbolisms is given in Chapter 13, The Wedding Rings.

In return for the engagement ring, it is usual for the bride-to-be to give her betrothed a gift, for example, a gold chain, tie clip or signet ring.

The Engagement Party

Engagement parties are held in order to make a public announcement, or simply to celebrate the good news and should be held soon after the decision is made to marry so that the event does not lose some of its excitement.

It is traditional for the bride's parents to arrange, organise and pay for the party. The mother of the bride-to-be sends out the invitations and has the choice to invite close family only, the whole family, or a mixture of family and friends. If she chooses the latter, great tact will need to be exercised so that any resentments are avoided.

Invitations to an engagement party need not be printed; they can be handwritten in the form of a letter, written on card, or a telephone call would suffice.

At a sit-down meal, the bride-to-be sits on the groom's left with her parents next to her; the groom's parents sit next to the groom. If parents are divorced, a tactful approach will be necessary and arrangements given much thought beforehand. It may be more tactful for the couple to celebrate with each set of parents separately.

If there are to be speeches at the party, it is usually the father of the bride-to-be who announces the engagement (if most of the guests are not already aware of the news) and wishes the couple health and happiness. The groom-to-be responds by proposing the health of both sets of parents.

Although engagement gifts are not expected, some family members will want to give something to mark the occasion.

Showers

Showers are parties or talk sessions strictly for females and are given by someone in honour of the bride-to-be. They are usually held during the daytime and at a friend's home.

The bride-to-be is consulted about the arrangements and provides the organiser with a list of those people whom she would like invited in accordance with a maximum number deemed by the organiser. Although the shower is given by the organiser, she does not have to know those invitees whom the bride selects.

At the shower, small gifts are offered to the bride and these normally have definite themes, for example, 'kitchen shower', 'all pink shower' to which all guests respond by donating a small appropriate item.

Following the shower, guests should write to the organiser thanking her for the occasion.

Deciding when to marry

There are a number of considerations when deciding when to marry, and setting the exact date may require some manoeuvring so that arrangements suit the diaries of the couple (taking into account any work or examination schedules for instance), the many special guests, and the bookings for the service, reception and honeymoon.

It is worth remembering that it is virtually impossible to arrange a formal wedding in less than six weeks and probably the minimum realistic length of time for an engagement should be three months.

Some religious denominations forbid marriages on certain days, specific dates or at certain times of the year. The appropriate officiant will be able to advise accordingly.

Time

Legally marriages may take place between 8 a.m. and 6 p.m. The only exceptions are Jewish and Quaker ceremonies and weddings performed under Special Licence or Registrar General's Licence.

Day

Weddings are generally not allowed in churches on Sundays and in Synagogues on the Jewish Sabbath (sundown Friday to sundown Saturday).

Register offices are closed on Saturday afternoons and on Sundays.

The day of the week on which the marriage takes place has superstition surrounding it, but despite this, most couples marry on Saturday and this is certainly more convenient for working guests. However, it is quite acceptable to have a week day wedding if this suits those concerned. Details concerning superstitions appear in Chapter 26, Wedding Customs.

Date

Legally marriages may take place on any date except Christmas Day.

Many brides favour a specific season but, particularly for a large or formal wedding, it is very important to allow sufficient time for preparations. The bride will also need to consider the convenience of the guests and avoid times when many are likely to be on holiday or when the weather may make travel difficult or impossible! It would be unfair to inflict long winter journeys on elderly or infirm relatives if this can be avoided.

It may be worth giving some thought to health aspects. Hay fever sufferers may wish to avoid certain months and those prone to bronchitis or flu may wish to avoid an autumn or winter wedding. If the bride suffers great discomfort at some particular time, it would be advisable to plan a date with this in mind. The wedding date may also depend on the choice and availability of the honeymoon.

Spring and summer weddings are the most popular seasons in which to get married generally because of the likelihood of good weather and the fact that these seasons suit both the work and holiday schedules for most people. If a winter wedding is considered, it should be remembered that afternoons become very dark at an early hour!

The tentative date will then have to suit the availability of venues: the church or register office and reception.

When a tentative date has been decided upon, it is necessary to ascertain the dates on which the church or register office is available.

Setting the Date

Year _____ Season _____ Month _____ Day _____

Dates to be avoided: Bride _____ Groom _____

Chosen date _____ Time _____

Availability of:

Best Man _____

Chief Bridesmaid _____

Bridesmaid _____

Bridesmaid _____

Bridesmaid _____

Flower Girl _____

Page Boy _____

Page Boy _____

Page Boy _____

Usher _____

Usher _____

Usher _____

Parents: Bride's _____

: Groom's _____

Church/Register Office _____

Notes _____

Honeymoon

Dates: From _____ To _____

Notes _____

Wedding Styles

There are many variations to the traditional weddings. Here is a sample.

Military

If one or both of the couple is in the forces, it may be desirable to have a military style wedding. If the groom is in the forces, he may wear his regulation uniform but a bride in the forces may prefer to wear traditional dress. Attending military personnel may also wear uniform.

Clergy

If the groom is a minister, the couple may choose to be married at his church rather than his fiancée's home church. The groom may wear his vestments and it is customary to invite the whole congregation to attend the wedding ceremony itself, although they do not have to be invited to the reception!

If a minister's son or daughter is to be married, he may conduct the ceremony in the chosen church if the resident minister agrees. Alternatively, it may be possible for the father to give the address.

Double

Double weddings can be very special occasions and usually take place when two siblings, twins or close friends decided to marry at the same ceremony and share the same reception. Double weddings can save much time, administration and reception costs, but on the other hand, specifics such as church processions and the order for speeches at the reception need very careful planning. A disadvantage may be that the brides have to share the limelight on the day, yet some couples may enjoy the celebrations more if they are not the sole centre of attention.

Where the brides are sisters, the elder takes precedence; if they are not, then the elder groom and his bride are attended to first. The father of sisters may proceed up the aisle with his daughters on either side. The couples may share attendants or they may have their own.

Although the number of attendants may have to be limited because of the size of the church, it is more practical to have two best men. Both grooms wait at the front of the church, each with his best man, and as the brides approach, the first groom moves to the centre of the aisle, with the second groom to his right.

The senior couple are first to take their vows and sign the register.

Where sisters are marrying, their mother is accompanied by the father of the first groom and their father with the mother of the first groom. The parents of the second groom are escorted by relations or close friends of the bride. The processional order and the escorts are largely a matter of personal preference; the important thing is that decisions are tactful so that no one is offended and that proceedings are fully rehearsed, understood and not forgotten.

Attendants must be careful that they maintain processional order and do not hamper the progress of the second bride. Obviously, it is important to hold at least one detailed rehearsal.

Breaking the Engagement

Broken engagements are inevitably a fact of life. Admitting a mistake takes courage and can be painful but a broken engagement is much less painful than a broken marriage. Relatives and friends can be informed quietly and should not expect an explanation.

It used to be possible to sue for breach of promise if one party broke off an engagement. It is not now possible to claim compensation for damaged feelings, or for the cost of incurred expenses such as invitations or attire. However, the couple can seek the help of the law if they are unable to agree on the division of any property that they may have purchased jointly. The rules of etiquette deem that if the bride-to-be breaks off the engagement, she should return the ring to the groom; if her fiancé breaks off the engagement, she is entitled to keep the ring, unless it is a family heirloom of course. In practice however, individual circumstances usually determine the fate of the ring. In an amicable parting, both parties may agree that the girl should keep the ring as a keepsake, or in other circumstances she may feel that it is more appropriate for the ring to be returned! Any gifts of value given to each other should be returned or at least offered.

Engagement gifts and any early wedding presents should be returned to donors as soon as possible after the engagement has been called off.

If the engagement has been formally announced in the newspaper, the girl's parents may insert a brief announcement:

> The marriage between
>
> Nel North
>
> and
>
> Sam South
>
> will not now take place

If the invitations have already been despatched, it is the responsibility of the girl or her parents, to cancel them. Formal invitations should be cancelled formally, for example:

> Mr and Mrs Ned North
>
> announce that
>
> the marriage of their daughter
>
> Nel
>
> to
>
> Mr Sam South
>
> will not now take place.

Ongoing Finances

Finances need to be organised carefully so that there are no disagreements about money and that the possibility of financial difficulties is minimised. Priorities should be established at an early stage and a simple budget devised covering the first year. This may then be adapted as circumstances change.

Assessments of income and expenditure should be honest; being realistic in advance prevents disappointments later!

If the income and expenditure totals do not balance, some adjustments will be necessary until a satisfactory and workable compromise is achieved.

Finances		
	£ per annum	£ per month
INCOME (net figures including overtime, bonuses, allowances, benefits, interest, etc.)		
Husband		
Wife		
Other		
TOTALS		

Finances (continued)		
	£ per annum	£ per month
EXPENDITURE **(including loan and hire purchase payments)**		
Household		
Mortgage/Rent		
House insurance		
Water rates		
Electricity		
Gas		
Solid fuel		
Telephone		
Television: repayments		
: licence		
Video repayments		
House maintenance		
House furnishings and fittings		
House decorations		
Household items		
Other		
Housekeeping		
Food and drink		
Cleaning		
Other		

Finances (continued)		
	£ **per annum**	**£** **per month**
EXPENDITURE		
Personal		
Life insurance		
Credit repayments		
Council tax		
Other		
Travelling/motoring		
Motor repayments		
Insurance		
Tax		
MOT		
Servicing		
Maintenance		
Petrol		
Public transport		
Other travelling expenses		
Attire and Accessories		
Wife		
Husband		
Dependants		

Finances (continued)		
	£ per annum	**£ per month**
EXPENDITURE		
Medical		
Cabinet		
Doctors		
Dentists		
Other		
Leisure		
Entertainment		
Hobbies		
Sport		
Club memberships		
Holidays		
Other		
Occasions		
Gifts: Birthdays		
Christmas		
Charities		
Other		

Finances (continued)		
	£ per annum	£ per month
EXPENDITURE		
Contingencies		
Savings		
Pensions		
Other		
TOTALS		

Totaliser		
	£ per annum	£ per month
Total Income		
Less: Total Expenditure		
Amount Remaining		

2 *What Kind of Wedding?*

THE FIRST and most important thing to do before you start your wedding planning is to decide whether you want a church or civil ceremony, and what kind of reception you would like. The first decision will depend on your religious beliefs, but the latter is very much a question of cost, so the first thing to do is set a budget.

Although traditionally the bride's father pays for most of the wedding, these days the bride and groom and the groom's parents often help to foot the bill. Whoever is paying, you will need a detailed budget to make sure you can afford the style of celebration you want.

The Estimated Budget

Your first step is to sit down with both families and work out an honest estimate of what each will contribute. And you need not limit your discussions to your parents if grandparents, godparents, aunts or uncles offer to pay a portion of the cost.

Then, by reading this book, talking to friends and generally looking around, you can work out roughly the type of wedding you would most like and an estimate of what it would cost. Be careful to compare like with like – for example, compare the cost of two similar bouquets using similar flowers – otherwise your comparisons will not be relevant and your estimate could be misleading. If this estimate does not fit your available funds, then begin to modify it until you have a wedding plan which you can keep within your budget.

Priorities

Everyone has strong opinions about how things should be done at a wedding. To one person, good food is the most important concern; to another having the best music is more significant. At this stage, you need to have an idea of your priorities; consider the items below and list them in order of their importance to you and your fiancé:

Reception venue; food; drink; music; photographer; invitations; wedding dress; groom's clothes; flowers; cake; other.

Once you decide which items to concentrate your expenditure on, you can begin to budget for the rest. Bear in mind that you cannot both have a different major expense as your first priority unless there is room in your budget. Avoid the pitfall of skimping on items that are actually a small fraction of the overall cost of the wedding.

The Final Plans

You can then make your final plans based on your budget. As each element becomes concrete, place the actual cost on your budget sheet. Make a note of deposits paid so that you have a full record of how your finances stand. If you find that you pay less for one service than you had anticipated, you may want to transfer that 'saving' to another area.

Try to allow five to ten per cent extra in your planning to allow for contingencies.

Don't forget to allow for the expenses of your new home, such as moving costs, deposits, installations and so on.

Agreements

Always deal with reputable companies and make written agreements where necessary for the services to be provided. Having the details in writing will be vital should an expected service not be provided, for example, and helps to clarify everything. Don't hesitate to ask questions and make sure you know exactly what is being provided, or what you are committing yourself to if you are signing an agreement.

3 Paying for the Wedding

THE COST of a large wedding would be well beyond the means of many families today if they had to pay for every part of it. Although it used to be traditional for the bride's family to pay for the wedding, this is not necessarily the case now. Many couples either pay for their own wedding, or contribute to the costs, and often the groom's family also contribute.

It may be helpful, however, to know who traditionally pays for the various expenses.

The Bride

Bridesmaids' dresses and gifts

Groom's ring and gift

Hen party

The Groom

Wedding ring

Wedding clothes

Legal and church costs

Bouquets for the bride and bridesmaids, coursages for the mothers and buttonholes for the principal men

Presents for the best man and ushers

Present for the bride

The stag party

Transport to the church for himself and the best man and to the reception for himself and the bride

The honeymoon

The Bride's Father

Wedding dress

Press announcements, invitations and stationery, and photographs

Flowers at the church and reception

Transport to the church for himself and the bride, the bride's mother and bridesmaids, and to the reception for himself and the bride's mother

The reception

The wedding cake

The Best Man

Own wedding clothes

4 The Legal Requirements

THIS CHAPTER deals with legal requirements you must fulfil when you wish to get married. It sounds very complicated, but that is only because there has to be a number of options to cater for all possibilities. If you have any queries or doubts, your minister or local registrar will be only too happy to explain what is the simplest and best way for you.

In any wedding, there are two declarations which must be made by both the bride and the groom.

'I do solemnly declare that I know not of any lawful impediment why I (full name) may not be joined in matrimony to (full name).'

'I call upon these persons here present to witness that I (full name) do take thee (full name) to be my lawful wedded wife/husband.'

England and Wales

In England and Wales a marriage can take place in a civil ceremony, a ceremony performed according to the rites of the Church of England or a ceremony performed according to the rites of any other religious denomination.

Church of England

There are four ways in which you can marry in the Church of England: by publication of banns; by common or ordinary licence; by special licence; by a licence issued by a Superintendent Registrar.

Generally, both bride and groom will be expected to be members of the Church of England and at least one of them should live in the parish of the church where the marriage is to take place, although exceptions are made, for example if you are marrying by special licence or if you are an established member of a church outside your home parish.

Publication of Banns
This is the most popular method. The first thing to do is to visit the minister of the church in which the marriage is to take place and ask him whether you can be married in his church. If you would like another minister to officiate at the wedding (an old friend of the family, for example) that should also be discussed. You may be expected to meet the minister several times to go through the ceremony to make sure that you fully understand the implications of your commitment. When all the preliminaries have been completed, the minister will publish the banns.

The banns are published by being read aloud in church on three successive Sundays preceding the ceremony. They are usually read at the main service. The couple usually attend church on at least one of the three occasions when the banns are read.

When the couple do not live in the same parish, the banns must be read in both parishes. A certificate confirming this must be obtained from the minister whose church is not being used for the ceremony to give to the officiating minister.

Once the banns have been published, the wedding can take place on any day within the following three months. If there is a delay for any reason, the banns will have to be called again.

If you are generally known by a name which is not on your birth certificate, the banns should give that name, or both. This is because the idea is to publicise the forthcoming marriage, and to substitute a misleading name is fraudulent.

Common or Ordinary Licence
This is a much quicker procedure since you need only one clear day's notice before the licence is issued and banns are unnecessary.

You can obtain a common licence from the Faculty Office, 1 The Sanctuary, Westminster, London SW1, or from the Bishop's Register Office (in any cathedral town) or from one of the Surrogates for granting licences in the diocese. If your minister does not hold this title himself, he will be able to tell you where you can obtain the licence in your particular area.

To obtain the licence, one of the couple must appear in person. They must sign a declaration that there is no legal reason why the marriage cannnot properly take place, and that one or both of them have lived for at least 15 days prior to the application in the parish of the church where they are to be married.

Special Licence

These are issued only by the Archbishop of Canterbury at the Faculty Office, 1 The Sanctuary, Westminster, London SW1 and are only used when there is some particular reason why the normal methods are unsuitable. When granted, a special licence allows the wedding to take place in any place, without residence restrictions, within three months of the date of issue.

Superintendent Registrar's Certificate

This method is very rarely used. The church where the marriage is to take place must be situated within the registration district of the Superintendent Registrar and one of the couple must have lived in the parish for seven days prior to giving notice.

The certificate will not be issued until 21 days after the notice is entered in the notice book and the ceremony may then take place within three months from the day on which the notice was entered. The marriage may be solemnised only by a minister of the Church of England and with the consent of the minister whose church is being used for the ceremony.

Before a Registrar

If you choose not to be married in a church, you can marry under civil law in a register office.

You will find the address of the local Superintendent Registrar in the telephone directory under 'Registration of Births, Marriages and Deaths'. Contact him to give notice of the marriage, and it will be arranged in one of three ways: Superintendent Registrar's Certificate; Superintendent Registrar's Certificate and Licence; Registrar General's Licence.

Superintendent Registrar's Certificate

The official will fill in a form giving the bride and groom's names and addresses, ages, and the location of the ceremony. There is a declaration to be signed which states that there is no legal objection to the marriage.

If both the man and the woman have lived in the area controlled by one registrar for seven days before giving notice only one of them need appear to make the declaration. If they live in different registration districts, they must each make the declaration before the registrar responsible for the district in which they live.

The Superintendent Registrar will make the entry in his notice book and issue the certificate 21 days later. The ceremony can then take place at any time within three months of the entry in the notice book. Remember that you have already used 21 days of this notice by the time you receive the certificate.

Superintendent Registrar's Certificate and Licence

A similar form and declaration have to be filled in for the certificate and licence, but the residence qualifications are different. Only one of the couple need give notice, even though they may live in different registration areas, provided that one of them has lived in the area for 15 days prior to the visit. However, the person not appearing must be within England and Wales or usually live there at the time the notice is given. The Superintendent Registrar will enter the notice and issue the licence for the marriage one clear day later. The licence is valid for three months.

Registrar General's Licence

This method was introduced in 1970 and is reserved for cases of extreme illness where it would be impossible for the marriage to take place in a register office or other registered building.

The licence permits the marriage to be solemnised in any place and at any time within three months from the date of entry in the notice book. There is no residence qualification and the licence can be issued immediately. Notice must be given in person by one of the couple to the local Superintendent Registrar.

Laws Governing Weddings

Once you have your licence, there are a number of other legal requirements to remember when making the arrangements for your wedding day.

1. Weddings cannot take place before 8.00 a.m. or after 6.00 p.m., except Jewish and Quaker ceremonies, and those performed with a Special Licence or a Registrar General's licence.

2. A wedding cannot be private, so the doors must not be locked while the ceremony is in progress.

3. You must hand all the relevant certificates or licences to the minister or registrar before the ceremony.

4. There must always be two people present at the ceremony who will sign their names as witnesses.

5. People under 16 years of age cannot marry. Couples between 16 and 18 must have the consent of their parents or guardians.

6. If one of the couple is already married, then the new marriage is invalid.

7. If either party is divorced, the marriage cannot take place until they have received the 'decree absolute'.

8. The couple must be male and female by birth.

9. Both parties must be acting by consent and be of sufficiently sound mind to understand the nature of the marriage contract.

10. Marriages are forbidden between people who are closely related, as listed below. If there is any doubt, consult your minister or Superintendent Registrar.

People You May Not Marry

Mother, adoptive or former adoptive mother
Mother's brother, sister, husband, mother or father
Mother's mother's husband, mother's father's wife

Father, adoptive or former adoptive father
Father's brother, sister, wife, mother or father
Father's mother's husband, father's father's wife

Daughter, adoptive or former adoptive daughter
Daughter's husband, son or daughter
Daughter's daughter's husband, daughter's son's wife

Son, adoptive or former adoptive son
Son's wife, son or daughter
Son's daughter's husband, son's son's wife

Sister, sister's son or daughter
Brother, brother's son or daughter

Wife's mother or daughter
Wife's mother's mother, wife's father's mother
Wife's son's daughter, wife's daughter's daughter

Husband's father or son
Husband's father's father, husband's mother's father.
Husband's son's son, husband's daughter's son

Other Denominations

If you wish to be married according to a religious denomination other than the Church of England, you must obtain a licence from the Superintendent Registrar as described above.

The building where the marriage is to take place must be registered for marriages, and the minister must be authorised to register the marriage. If he is not, the registrar must be present.

Scotland

The rules governing weddings are slightly different under Scottish law, and are governed by The Marriage (Scotland) Act 1977.

You can be married by a registrar, or assistant registrar, and the wedding will normally be held in his office. Alternatively, you can be married by any clergyman who is entitled to undertake marriages under the Act. Whatever type of wedding you have, there must be at least two witnesses who are 16 years of age or over.

First, obtain a marriage notice form from a

registrar of births, marriages and deaths in Scotland. His address will be in the telephone directory. Both the bride and groom must fill in a form with their name and address, sex and marital status. You must confirm that you are not closely related in any way that forbids marriage. The forms must be signed, and if any of the information given is incorrect, the marriage will not be valid.

If either of you has been married before, the forms must be completed at least six weeks before the ceremony. Otherwise they should be completed about a month before (15 days is the minimum). The forms must be returned to the registrar for the district where the ceremony is to take place. He will also require your birth certificate. If either of you have been married before, you will also have to produce a death certificate of your former spouse, or a copy of the divorce decree. If either bride or groom lives outside the United Kingdom, you must produce documentation, in a certified translation if necessary, that there are no reasons in your own country why you should not be married.

The registrar will then prepare a marriage schedule. If the ceremony is to be in his office, he will keep this until the wedding. If it is to be held elsewhere, one of you must collect it in person not more than a week before the wedding. After the ceremony, the schedule must be signed by the bride and groom, two witnesses and the minister who conducted the wedding. Return this to the registrar within three days.

Don't forget that you must also make the arrangements with the church or register office where the ceremony is to take place.

If one of you lives in Scotland and the other in England or Wales, the one in Scotland should give notice in the normal way. The one in England should give notice to the Superintendent Registrar where he or she lives. Notices issued in England and Wales are valid in Scotland and vice-versa, as long as only one of the couple lives in Scotland. Marriage by licence in a register office in England or Wales, however, is not possible in this case.

Northern Ireland

In order to get married in Northern Ireland you must give notice to the District Registrar of Marriages for the District in which you have been resident for at least the last seven days. The marriage can then take place by licence, special licence, certificate from a registrar, licence from a District Registrar of Marriages or the publication of banns.

Notices issued in Northern Ireland are valid in England and Wales and vice-versa, but as in Scotland, you cannot marry in a register office in England or Wales if one of you lives in Northern Ireland.

Canada

The legal requirements and procedures for marriage differ from one province to another. It is therefore very important to establish exactly how to make the correct arrangements, and to do this you should ask at the Registry Office at your local Town Hall.

United States of America

As in Canada, the law relating to marriage is different in different States. It is very important to find out the correct requirements and procedures in your State, and you should therefore ask as soon as possible at the office of the Clerk of the Circuit Court. Every State requires a licence before a marriage can take place. In most cases these must be obtained at least 1 to 5 days before the date set for your wedding, and will expire 30 days after they are issued – so you must get your timing right. The licence must be signed by two witnesses, and you must keep it very safely once you are married.

All States now require both bride and groom to have a blood test before they can marry, and some make further stipulations as to medical testing. Be sure to allow sufficient time for these procedures to be gone through.

5 The Best Man, Bridesmaids and Wedding Party

CHOOSING your special attendants is a way of surrounding yourself on your wedding day with those people who are closest to you. They act as helpers in all sorts of capacities, and add to the general atmosphere of enjoyment.

For the bride, her attendants are her chief bridesmaid and other bridesmaids; the groom chooses a best man and ushers. The number of attendants is entirely up to you. Every wedding requires at least two witnesses, but you may prefer to ask your parents to fulfil this role. You can choose anyone you wish, although family members are generally the first to be selected, and it is thoughtful to include people from both the bride's and the groom's families. Close friends are also often included.

You probably already have a good idea of the people you would like to ask. Many brides find the difficulty is not being able to ask everyone. Don't feel obliged to ask someone to be one of your attendants purely because you were one of theirs. This is not expected. However, if there are people you are unable to include, try to explain the problem to them and they will probably be most understanding. You could perhaps ask them to fulfil some other special role.

Ask your chosen friend whether they would like to be your best man or bridesmaid. They will most probably be honoured, but they could be a little overawed by the responsibility, especially if it is a big wedding. Take time to chat with them informally so that they know what is expected of them. If you want them to take on certain duties, such as providing transport on your wedding day, ask them; don't expect them to guess what they should be doing.

It is customary for the bride and groom to give a gift to the bridesmaids and best man either at the pre-wedding parties, or on the morning of the wedding. Some items can be personalised with your names and the wedding date if you wish. Jewellery is a popular and special gift.

Chief Bridesmaid

You usually choose a sister or close friend, since the chief bridesmaid acts as adviser, messenger and general assistant to the bride. The chief bridesmaid is known as the matron of honour if she is married.

She will assist you as much as possible in the wedding planning and preparation and attend the pre-wedding festivities whenever possible. You may ask her to help you choose your wedding dress and the dresses for herself and the other bridesmaids.

On the wedding day, she will be near you throughout the day. She will probably help you to dress and do your hair and make-up. She will leave for the church with the other bridesmaids and your mother, then wait for you at the church.

At the church, she will make sure your dress and veil are perfect, and will follow you and your father up the aisle to the chancel steps where she will take your bouquet. If you wear a veil, she will help to lift it back at the appropriate moment. She will follow on the arm of the best man into the vestry where you sign the register, and you may ask her to be a witness. She will return your bouquet to you before you leave the vestry, and follow you out of the church with the best man.

Throughout the day, she will look after the bridesmaids, especially the younger ones, making sure that they are looked after and that they are behaving themselves. There will usually be plenty of family and friends to help her, but a watching brief is never a bad idea.

She will also have a watching brief on the bride, making sure that she looks her best, is supplied with tissues if necessary, or perhaps a comb or make-up. You may ask her to keep a handbag handy with any bits and pieces which you make need during the day: tissues, make-up, comb, safety pins, hair clips and so on.

At the reception, she will join the receiving line, and can be generally helpful in circulating with the guests and helping you to make sure that everyone is enjoying themselves. When it is time for you to leave, she will help you to change, and will usually look after your dress, taking it home or returning it to the shop if it is hired.

Bridesmaids and Page Boys

The bridesmaids complete the beautiful picture of the bride, and help her whenever they are needed. If the bridesmaids are very young, remember that someone should be nearby to keep an eye on them and look after them.

You can, of course, choose page boys as well as bridesmaids if you have relations or sons of friends who would like to attend you at the wedding.

Best Man

The best man is the groom's assistant for the wedding, and is usually his brother or close friend. He reassures the groom when he is nervous, and is there to give support and help whenever needed. He is an organiser. You should rely on him to handle details such as making sure the ushers are in the right place at the right time and are correctly dressed. He usually arranges the stag party for the groom, helps him dress the morning of the wedding and gets him to the church at least 15 minutes before the service is due to start. Make sure he knows exactly how long the journey will take in the traffic conditions at that time of the day.

At the church, he will make sure the ushers know their duties, and will distribute the buttonholes and corsages as the principal guests arrive. If there are order of service sheets, he should make sure that he collects them before the day and has them ready for distribution to the guests. He takes care of the ring and the marriage licence and can be a witness on it. The groom can give the best man whatever fees and gratuities there are to be paid, thus relieving himself of additional responsibilities.

The best man is responsible for getting the bridesmaids and guests safely from the church to the reception, so he should check in advance who is escorting whom and make any necessary arrangements. Having a few telephone numbers of taxi firms ready is a good idea in case anyone is unexpectedly without transport.

At the reception, he will join the receiving line, and can be generally useful in talking with the guests and making sure they are all enjoying themselves. Once the dancing starts, he is often expected to dance with as many partners as possible.

Probably what most best men dread most is the speech he is expected to make at the reception, although this need not be such an ordeal if a little planning and forethought go into it. First he has to respond to the toast to the bridesmaids, given by the groom. He can find out what the groom intends to say if that helps, so that he has a suitable response. Generally, the groom will make a few complimentary remarks, so the best man can agree and add a few of his own, especially if he is single. The next part of his speech usually involves some reminiscence about the groom, or perhaps about when the bride and groom first met. It should be light-hearted and preferably humorous, but never cause embarrassment either to the bride and groom or to the guests. Telling a joke is only a good idea if the best man is a good joke-teller, and if the choice is suitable for the occasion. Anything which is likely to be told after 10 o'clock at the stag party is unlikely to be suitable for the wedding reception. Finally, he reads the congratulatory telegrams, or a selection if there are too many to read them all.

If there is a display of gifts at the bride's parents' home, he usually arranges to transport guests to see them.

He makes sure that the groom's car is ready at the reception for when the couple leave, and is generally the one who arranges to decorate the car. Make sure he knows that shaving foam can damage paintwork! He should make sure that the groom has all the necessary travel documents for the honeymoon, as well as his suitcase and the bride's suitcase.

Ushers

You generally have as many ushers as you have bridesmaids. They arrive early at the church to distribute the order of service sheets and show the guests to their seats. They also escort the bridesmaids during the day. As a general idea, you will need about one usher for every 50 guests. They can help to ensure that all the guests are safely transported from the church to the reception, and the best man may ask one to remain behind to check for any property left in the church.

The Bride's Parents

The bride's parents are the hosts of the wedding. They will help in all aspects of the planning and arrangements. They send out the invitations and receive the replies, and the presents are usually sent to their home.

The bride's mother should choose her outfit well in advance, including all the accessories. It is customary for her to let the groom's mother know what she will be wearing so that they can avoid colour clashes!

On the day, the bride's mother travels to the church with the bridesmaids and is the last to take her place in the church. She goes into the vestry on the arm of the groom's father, and leaves the church with him.

The bride's father escorts his daughter to the chancel steps and stands just behind her during the ceremony. He escorts the groom's mother to the vestry and from the church.

The bride's parents are first in the receiving line at the reception and host the occasion. They are also usually responsible for making sure all the guests leave safely and the clearing-up is attended to.

After the wedding, the bride's mother usually takes care of the gifts and organises the distribution of photograph proofs and the collection of orders. She may also send out pieces of cake to those who did not attend the wedding.

The Groom's Parents

It makes for the best atmosphere if the two sets of parents have met and made friends before the wedding. Usually, they co-operate in the arrangements and the finances.

They sit at the front of the church on the groom's side, and join the wedding party when they go to sign the register. They usually join the receiving line at the reception.

Special Situations

If there are cases of death or divorce in the family, the situation should be handled tactfully and with understanding to suit the circumstances involved.

If either set of parents are divorced and remarried, the mother sits in the first pew with her new partner, and the father and his new partner take the second pew on the relevant side of the church. The receiving line at the reception includes the host and hostess of the reception – usually the bride's mother and father – and the groom's mother and father. New partners are not normally included in the receiving line. Seating at the top table should be handled tactfully, with everyone given a place if possible.

6 The Announcements

EVERYONE wants to share the news of their engagement and wedding with both family and friends.

Engagement Announcements

Naturally, you will have told both sets of parents of your engagement first of all. Most people also like to tell close relatives and friends personally or by telephone. Many people write to other relations and friends announcing their engagement and giving a few details about their fiancé and their future plans. If you do this, it is a good idea to post all the letters together so that no one feels left out of the exciting news.

Some people choose to announce their engagement in the national papers, but for most an announcement in their local paper is a good way of letting neighbours and casual friends know about their engagement. Many papers have a standard form for you to fill in. Whether you are writing out your announcement or filling in a form, write clearly and legibly and make sure all the names are spelled correctly.

Wedding Announcements

In much the same way, most couples like to announce their wedding in the local papers so that any casual friends may, if they like, join in wishing them well at the church or register office, for example, or send them a card.

Check the date you need to send in your announcement for it to appear in the appropriate edition and send in the details in plenty of time. Either write them out clearly or use the form provided by the newspaper if they prefer. Don't try to include too much information because it will probably be cut out if there is limited space. Something along these lines is suitable.

Mr and Mrs John Smith
are pleased to announce the marriage of
their daughter
Sarah Jane to
Mr Peter Brown
at 2 p.m.
on Saturday 15 June 19--
at St Mary's Church, High Street, Reading.
All friends welcome at the church.

If there are people you would particularly like to know about your marriage, but your guest list is limited and you cannot invite them to the wedding, a personal letter is probably the best way to let them know the news in a friendly way.

After the wedding, many couples like their photograph to appear in the local paper, and most local newspapers have a form which you fill in and send to them with an appropriate picture. It contains details of the bride and groom, where they were married, where they met, their destination on honeymoon, the bride's dress and attendants and so on. Fill it in well in advance and keep it in a safe place. It is a good idea to delegate someone else – probably your mother – to send it to the paper with a photograph immediately after the wedding.

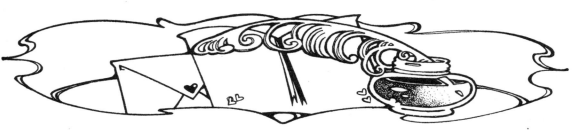

7 The Guest List

SHARING your happiness on your wedding day with those closest to you is all part of the enjoyment.

Preparing your guest list may not be as easy as you think, since you must be guided by your budget and the style of your wedding, and may not be able to ask as many people as you would wish. As a general guide, expect at least 75 per cent of those invited to attend.

Draft List

The first thing to do is set the total number. By tradition (because they used to pay for everything), the bride's family sets the size of the guest list. The best way to do this is to sit down with your parents and make a draft list in three categories: definite, probable, possible. List your relations and close friends first under the appropriate heading, then go through other friends, neighbours, colleagues, double-checking to make sure you have not forgotten anyone. Don't be tempted to invite acquaintances, otherwise your list will soar. Then (or at the same time) consult the groom and his parents. However many you decide on, the bride usually has half and the groom half. If the bride's family is three times larger than the groom's, then a tactful compromise will have to be worked out.

Before you finalise your list, decide what you will do in the following situations to avoid possible embarrassment. If you are having a small wedding, most people understand that the guest list will be limited, but it can be more difficult for a large wedding.

1. If an invited guest asks to bring a friend. Numbers can add up quickly if you are not careful – a few more, even in a large crowd, makes a substantial difference.

2. If you have 20 cousins, but are only close enough to one or two of them to really want to invite to the wedding, do you invite them all to avoid hurt feelings?

3. Will you be inviting children to the wedding? You should make this clear on the invitation, and either decide on an 'adult' wedding or invite all the children.

Keep the draft list to refer to in case a number of guests are unable to come and you wish to send a few more invitations.

Preparing the List

You can then make your final guest list, including names, addresses and telephone numbers. If you make it an invitation and present list, you will have all the addresses to hand when you come to write your thank you letters. Remember to invite the clergyman, and perhaps his wife if he is married.

There is no need to include everyone who gives you a present. Send them a thank you and plan to invite them for dinner after the wedding. Once the list is complete, check it for duplicates or last-minute additions.

When you have the complete list, check to see whether anyone has special needs which you should take account of. Are any of your guests vegetarian, or do they have any other special dietary requirements? Will you need any highchairs for children, or to make any arrangements for a disabled guest?

You may also like to make a note of anyone you cannot invite, but would like to write to personally, to tell them the good news.

Unless everyone is local, it can be a good idea to draw a small map of the location of the church or register office and the venue of the reception so no one gets lost.

Guests Travelling to the Wedding

Although you are not responsible for lodging or transport for people travelling to the wedding, it would be helpful to provide them with information about hotels in your area, their rates and so on. It might be appropriate for all your guests to stay in one place, so you can arrange a group discount.

8 Invitations and Stationery

BY NOW, the wedding arrangements are falling into place and your guest list is finalised. About three months before the wedding, you should choose your invitations.

Styles of Invitations

The type of invitation you choose will give your guests a clue to what style of wedding you will have. For a small, informal wedding, a handwritten invitation on attractive stationery is fine. For a larger wedding, you will probably choose to have them printed. The choice of styles is vast, so take your time looking through the printer's catalogue to choose a style which suits. Black is the traditional colour for the lettering.

You may want to be really original and design your own invitations. If you are good at calligraphy, now's your chance to get into print! Or you may like to design a monogram or even a small illustration for your cards. Shop around and find a local printer who will give you guidance and help so that you can create a really professional job.

Ordering

Make sure you give the printer all the correct details. Double-check dates, times and names in particular as it is easy to make mistakes.

When calculating the number of invitations to order, check that you have:

one for each couple or family;
one for each single adult;
enough for the bridesmaids and attendants;
one for the clergyman if you are inviting him to the reception;
a few extras for yourselves and your parents as souvenirs;
some spares for the last minute addition of forgotten guests, or guests to be invited if others are unable to attend;
a few invitations to replace any that get lost or damaged.

Wording

Invitations are traditionally sent by the bride's parents, since they will normally be the hosts at the wedding. The invitations are usually written formally, in the third person. For example:

Mr and Mrs Thomas Jones
request the pleasure of the company of

_____

at the marriage of their daughter
Patricia Jane
to
Mr Robert Stephen Smith
at St. Joseph's Church
Church Road, Marlow
on Saturday 18 June 19--
at 2.30 p.m.
and afterwards at a reception at
The Rose Inn, Marlow

RSVP
37 Milton Road
Marlow
Buckinghamshire

The bride's surname is not normally included, but it can be appropriate if it differs from that of the host and hostess.

The exact wording will vary if the bride's mother is a widow, or her parents are divorced, for example.

Mrs Thomas Jones
requests the pleasure of the company of

If you are inviting guests to the ceremony, but not to the reception, then the wording should be altered accordingly. Alternatively, you may ask some guests to the ceremony, then to a party in the evening. It should be quite clear what invitation you are extending, and in some cases it may be worth preparing two separate invitations.

If it is to be a double wedding, the older of the two couples, or the bride who is closest in relationship to the host and hostess should be mentioned first.

Checking the Invitations

The printer will supply you with a proof of the invitations for you to check before he prints them. Make sure you check the following points.

1. Is the card or paper the right colour and quality?
2. Is the lettering style correct?
3. Are the borders or designs correct?
4. Are the dates and times accurate?
5. Are all the names spelled correctly?
6. Are the addresses correct?
7. Are the commas and apostrophes in the right places?
8. Will they be ready on time?
9. Have you ordered the right quantity?

Addressing the Invitations

When you receive the invitations, fill them in clearly with the names of those invited, including the children, address and stamp the envelopes and send them all at the same time. Don't forget to include maps if you have prepared them or information on local hotels where necessary. Do not be tempted to send them in batches as this may offend someone who receives a 'late' invitation.

Replies and Extra Invitations

Formal replies should be sent within three days of receiving the invitation, so you should quickly have a more definite idea of your numbers. You may be able to send out a few more invitations should a number of guests be unable to attend. Mark acceptances and refusals on your guest list as you receive them.

Other Stationery and Souvenirs

There is a vast choice of other stationery which you can have personally printed for your wedding. It may be very attractive, but is expensive and is certainly not essential, so consult your budget carefully before you are tempted to order things you do not really need.

Seating Cards

These can be useful so that everyone knows where to sit at the reception. You could, of course, make your own from white card. An overall seating plan is usually prepared as well, but it is easier for guests to find their seats if cards are supplied.

Thank You Cards

These can be personally printed so that you merely have to sign them and address the envelope. Although such cards make it very easy for you, they will give far less pleasure than a personally written thank you note.

Cake Boxes

Many people like to send a small piece of cake to people who were unable to attend the wedding.

Order of Service Sheets

You may like to have the wedding service printed so that it is easy for your guests to follow. The stationer will probably have a sample design on which you can base your details. Check these with the minister to make sure everything is correct. You may not be singing all the verses of the chosen hymn, for example.

Miscellaneous

If you can afford to be really extravagant, you can have serviettes, ashtrays, matchbooks or other souvenirs printed with your names and the date of your wedding.

9 Your Wedding Dress and the Bridesmaids' Dresses

YOU MAY already have a picture in your mind of the dress you would most like for your wedding, or you may have a dozen ideas. This chapter will help you to choose.

Of course you will want to take your time when making such an important choice. You will be choosing a complete outfit, which can be very expensive whether you buy or hire. The style of your dress will also set the tone for other members of the wedding party.

There are a number of choices open to you. You can buy a dress from a bridal shop, where they offer a range of beautiful gowns from which to choose. You can go to a salon and have a dress made for you – an expensive choice which is out of the question for most brides. You can make your own dress or have it made by a friend or a local dressmaker. You can borrow a dress from your sister or friend, wear one that your grandmother wore, or you can often buy beautiful dresses second-hand. Or you may choose to hire a dress for that special day.

Wedding dresses can be very expensive, so think carefully about how much you want to spend. You want to look wonderful, of course, but remember that most wedding dresses are worn just for the one day, so you may prefer to spend less on your wedding dress and use the money for some new clothes for the honeymoon. Many brides who buy expensive wedding dresses, regret it later when they see it hanging in the spare wardrobe. Hand-finishing, special fabrics and trimmings all add to the cost, so a polyester dress will be less expensive than a silk or satin one, but may look equally wonderful.

Choosing the Best Style

If you have a perfect figure and complexion, then the choice is all yours, but for most brides, different styles can be more or less flattering. Don't opt for a style simply because it is the most fashionable if it does not suit you.

If you are short, you can add to your apparent height by choosing a neat style, perhaps with a bell skirt, and a design with vertical lines of appliqué. If you also select a dress with some delicate detail around the neck and shoulders, the eyes of those watching you will inevitably be raised to your upper half.

Those who are on the tall side will want to reverse the effect just described. They should therefore choose a dress with a flounced skirt and a simple, low neckline. Taller brides should also take care to avoid an elaborate headdress which will obviously add further height.

If you would like to appear more curvaceous, choose a dress with a full, softly gathered skirt and full, long sleeves, in a gently draping fabric. You can still accentuate your slender waist by wearing a pretty sash or by choosing a fitted bodice.

For brides with a fuller figure a simple, well fitting dress is very important. Above all, do not be tempted to get a dress that is too tight. Particular problem areas can often be hidden by choosing the right style. For example, if you have a thick waist you should wear a high waisted or a-line dress. If your hips are large, stick to an a-line skirt and add detail elsewhere, at the neck or shoulders for instance. Brides with broad shoulders should avoid drawing attention to them, by choosing a simple neckline or a wide draping collar. If your bosom is large, avoid high waistlines that gather under the bust, and choose a neckline that draws the eye away from the bust.

Whatever your shape or size, you can be a beautiful bride if you choose a dress that makes the most of your good features and disguises or glides simply over those of which you are less proud.

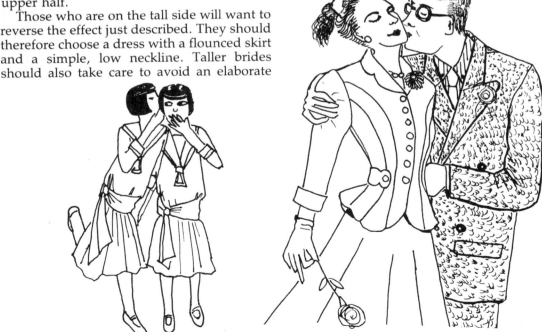

Trimmings

There are many finishing touches which can transform a simple dress into a stunning one, as well as help to accentuate your best features and gloss over those you are not so proud of.

Fabric, silk or lace flowers can be dotted over the dress, or larger flowers can be used to emphasise a scooped hemline, decorate a sash or add interest to a plain bodice.

Lace can be used in all sorts of ways for panels, round necklines or sleeves, for underskirts or as a fine layer over a different fabric.

Ribbons can be used to highlight embroidery or emphasise clever shaping on a dress. They can be tied in sashes or bows to decorate a simple hem, neckline or sleeve.

Embroidery can be used in panels, to highlight parts of the dress or as an all-over effect. Pintucks can give an elegant, Victorian look to a fitted bodice.

Frills, flounces and ruffles are very popular in wedding dresses because they make the dress look so different from even the most sophisticated evening dress and give a really old-fashioned feminine effect.

Shopping for your Dress

It is a good idea to have a look at magazines so that you know roughly what style of dress you want before you start visiting shops, otherwise you can be bewildered by the choice. The most important things to consider, after cost, are whether the style suits you and makes you look your best, and whether it is comfortable. You don't want to be thinking about a tight bodice while you are standing at the chancel steps, or worrying that you might split your sleeve if you dance too energetically at the reception!

Allow plenty of time to look round, and go for a window-shopping trip first, with no intention of buying. That way you will avoid feeling rushed into a hasty decision.

When you go to buy your dress, tell the assistant your budget, and remember that you may want a headdress and veil, shoes and underwear as well. Only look at the dresses in your price range, or you may be tempted to extravagance and regret it afterwards. Take your mother or chief bridesmaid along for a second opinion. They know you well enough to help you select a dress that suits you, and can offer advice and suggestions as well as sharing in the excitement.

To make sure the dress looks and feels right, try it on. It should reflect your personality and enhance your best features. Take time to study the effect of the dress on you, and try it on with the headdress you have chosen to see the overall effect. Wear your wedding shoes or ones with a similar heel to check the length and that the hemline falls perfectly. Make sure it is well made, flatters your figure, feels comfortable and moves well. Don't forget the back of the dress – that is what the guests will see during the ceremony. Don't be rushed, and try on as many as you like.

Most wedding dresses are white, ivory or cream. Choose your colour carefully and make sure that it does not wash all the colour out of your skin.

Hiring a Dress

If you decide to hire a dress, the procedure is the same as buying. Choose the complete outfit as early as possible from the hire firm, then book it for your wedding day. Find out when you will be able to collect the dress and when it should be returned. Your mother or chief bridesmaid can do this for you if you are going away on honeymoon. Make sure you know when the balance of the hire charge is payable – you will probably have to pay a deposit – and whether you are responsible for having the dress cleaned. Normally the hire firm arranges this.

Buying Second-Hand

You may be able to buy a dress at an agency, or through a personal advertisement. Many beautiful bargains can be picked up this way. Start looking early, and don't be embarrassed into buying a dress you are not sure about. If you ring before visiting someone with a dress for sale, chat to them about the style and the fit so you have a good idea of the dress before you go to see it.

Making your Dress

Unless you are an experienced dressmaker, it is probably best not to attempt to make your wedding dress. It will be much harder to make than an ordinary day dress, and the standards you set for the finished result will be very high.

For those who are able to sew well, however, this is a great option, for you can create your own style either by designing your own pattern, or by adjusting a bought pattern to suit your own ideas. You can feel really proud of yourself as you walk down the aisle.

Here are a few tips which are worth remembering, even if you are a very experienced dressmaker.

1. Don't choose a pattern which is beyond your capabilities.

2. Choose a fabric which you will enjoy working on; some are more difficult than others.

3. Make up the dress in a cheap fabric first so that you can make all the fit and style adjustments before you cut into expensive fabric.

4. Store the garment carefully while you are working on it. Keep it in a large plastic bag or inside a duvet cover.

5. Make sure you have all the right equipment and materials for decorating the dress.

6. Have someone else help you with fittings; it is almost impossible to fit a dress on yourself.

7. Allow plenty of time.

8. If you doubt your abilities, buy a ready-to-sew kit.

Does the Dress Fit?

It is very important to make sure that your dress fits properly, otherwise it will not be comfortable and you will not look your best.

Fitted styles should be well tailored and fit snugly, but should not be too tight. If the dress pulls out of shape anywhere, this is a sure sign that it needs alteration. Make sure that the waistline is correct. It will feel awkward if too high, and will crease round the middle if it is too low. The shoulders should not be too wide, and the armholes should allow room for comfortable movement. A high neck should fit neatly and not push up under the chin; a rounded neckline should not be loose.

The key to correctly-fitting sleeves is comfort and ease of movement. Long tightly-fitting sleeves are probably not the best choice because they will restrict arm movements. A long sleeve should fall to your wrist, with any lace or trim extending over your upper hand.

The dress should be about 5 cm off the floor when you are wearing your shoes so that the skirt does not drag on the ground. The dress should hang beautifully and move with you when you walk.

If you are having a custom-made dress, you will need enough time to arrange several fittings and for alterations if necessary, so start shopping as early as possible.

Bear in mind that you may gain or lose some weight before the day, so allow for this when fitting.

Headdress and Veil

Your headdress is a very important part of your costume. Try it on while wearing the dress so that you can see the total effect, and wear your hair how you think you will want to wear it on the day as this will change the look. Choose a headdress or hat that complements the style of your dress, your facial features and hairstyle. Whatever particular decorative features your dress has, those of your headdress should blend with and complement it.

Your veil must also of course match your style of dress and headdress; the only way to tell is to try them on. Generally speaking, the more formal your dress, the longer your veil can be, but the most important thing is to find what looks best. If you also choose a blusher veil, worn over your face for the processional, the chief bridesmaid will help you to move it back for the ceremony.

You may, of course, choose not to wear a veil; there are plenty of other options. You may want a small hat or cap, perhaps with a veil. Beware of hats with large brims which will shade your face in the photographs and knock into the bridegroom when you turn round! You could wear a circlet of flowers, or ribbons trimmed with flowers. These can look wonderful with a fall of lace. You may want to wear a tiara, although this would really go best with a formal dress in which case you would wear it with a full veil. Or you may just choose a few flowers to wear in your hair.

Accessories

The colour of your underwear must be chosen with great care to avoid any shadows showing through your dress. The styles of your bra and slip are also very important, and the wise bride will experiment and take advice to find which will set off her dress to most advantage. Whether you wear tights or stockings, they should be sheer and either completely see through or the same colour as your dress.

If you need any special underwear such as a crinoline petticoat, investigate hiring or borrowing before you buy.

Buy your shoes well in advance to match your dress in colour and style. Remember that you will be wearing them all day and will be standing and dancing much of the time, so if you are not comfortable in a high heel, choose a lower one. Break them in before the wedding day, and make sure any tickets are removed from the sole. If they have a smooth sole, make sure you have worn them outside to scratch the surface so that you don't slip.

Keep jewellery very simple so that it does not draw attention away from your dress. A simple locket, gold chain or a strand of pearls are the most popular. If you wear earrings, make sure they are the right size and proportion to suit your headdress.

There is no need to wear gloves unless you are having a very formal wedding and they are never worn with long sleeve dresses. If you do want to wear them, choose fingerless gloves or have the ring finger slit so that you do not have to remove your whole glove when your hand will probably be shaking.

You can buy a handbag to match your dress to carry personal items such as make-up, comb, tissues, safety pins, perfume and so on, although you might prefer to buy a handbag to match your going-away outfit since it will probably be tucked away for emergencies and not on display with your dress. Some brides carry fans, parasols or other things on their wedding day, but remember that you will have your bouquet to carry, and other items may be a nuisance. Just in case, it is not a bad idea to borrow a pretty umbrella for the day and hope to leave it at home! Sometimes chauffeurs or photographers carry large white umbrellas with them; find out in advance.

Hair and Make-Up

Practise your hair several times before the day if you are doing it yourself, or ask the hairdresser to do a trial run, especially if you are choosing a more elaborate style than usual. Try your headdress on with the right hair style for the full effect. As with everything about your dress for the special day, remember that you want to look beautiful and feel comfortable, so if you hate wearing your hair on top, don't, otherwise it will detract from your enjoyment. Also work out how you will adapt the style, if necessary, to suit your going-away outfit.

It is best to keep make-up low-key and natural looking, especially with white or pale dresses. Experiment in advance, and drape a white towel round your shoulders or wear a white blouse so that you can see the effect. Go for something very similar to your usual make-up. Invest in a spot cover-up stick, just in case.

Many experts recommend wearing a foundation that is slightly lighter than you normally use, with pink undertones if your dress is white or cream. Apply a little pink or plum blusher to the cheekbones, temples and the bridge of your nose, and finish with a matt powder. It is best to choose a clear shade of eyeshadow, and if you are using eyeliner you should select a colour which goes well with your eyeshadow. Avoid a dark eyeliner because it will appear too theatrical in the photographs. Your lipstick should be a light or bright plum or pink, rather than any shade of brown or orange which tend to look faded in photographs.

Remember that everyone will want to look at your rings, so your hands will receive extra attention. Treat yourself to a manicure a week before the wedding and keep your nails carefully shaped. Use plenty of hand cream if your hands tend to be rough. Choose a suitable nail varnish for the day; something subtle is usually best with a white or cream dress.

Looking your Best

If you feel you need to lose some weight before the wedding, set yourself a realistic target, start early, and concentrate on getting into a routine of healthy eating rather than trying crash diets, then putting the weight back on again. If you lack the will power, join a slimming club to gain some moral support.

Try to get plenty of sleep, especially the week before the wedding, so you have plenty of energy. And if you want to indulge in a sauna, a facial or professional hair removal, arrange it at least a week before the big day just in case you have any reaction to the treatment.

On the Day

Very few brides are not nervous on their wedding day, so be prepared. It is a wonderful and emotional day and you will be the centre of attention, so it is very rare to go through the whole day calm and serene. If you know you will cry, bring plenty of tissues and make-up for touching-up. Take a comb, especially if you have a headdress to remove for the reception, some safety pins and anything else you think you might need. The chief bridesmaid can be in charge of your handbag of bits and pieces.

If you have a long train on the dress, work out how you will wear it at the reception to keep it out of the way and avoid spoiling it. Also take care when getting into and out of cars to ensure that everything is inside and nothing is catching in the door.

Preserving your Dress and Veil

If you have a less formal style of dress, you may want to have it dyed or altered so that you can wear it again. Or, you may want to sell it, loan it to others, or keep it for your daughter. The following ideas are suggestions for keeping the dress at its most beautiful, although results cannot be guaranteed.

Take the dress to a good dry cleaner. Make sure that they will not add starch or sizing to the dress, as this will attract damaging bugs.

Once it has been cleaned, remove it from the plastic bag and take out the metal hanger and any pins or tape which the cleaner has attached. Hang it on a padded, unscented hanger which has been wrapped in clean muslin. Leave it to air thoroughly until there is no longer any smell of cleaning fluid. Stuff any bouffant parts of the dress with acid-free tissue paper so they keep their shape. Buy some unbleached cotton muslin and wash it several times in hot water. Make a muslin bag for the dress and store it in a clean, dry place. Never use pins or sticky tape to seal the bag as they may damage the fabric.

The best way to clean a veil is to wash it in the bath. Remove it from the headdress and mend any tears. Again using unbleached cotton muslin which has been washed and well-rinsed, tack the veil to a piece of muslin. Fill the bath to about 10 cm deep with lukewarm water and a soapless detergent. Put the veil in the water and very gently rub it clean with your fingers. Be careful not to twist or wring it. Leave the veil in the bath while you drain the soapy water and refill with lukewarm rinsing water. Rinse about three times, then drain. Press excess water out of the veil with a white (or matching) towel, then lift it out of the bath onto a dry matching towel, cover with another matching towel and press out as much water as possible, keeping the towels flat. Then lay the veil on a dry towel in front of a breezy window. Avoid direct sunlight. When it is completely dry, roll the veil (with the muslin still attached) and cover it with acid-free tissue paper. Store in a bag similar to the one made for the dress.

Your Trousseau

The trousseau dates from the days when a bride took with her enough clothing and household linen to last at least a year. Nowadays, this is not necessary, although many brides like to start a 'bottom drawer', buying things gradually for their new home. It is also nice to have some new clothes, especially if you are going away on honeymoon.

If you are choosing new clothes, try not to be extravagant on things that will not get much wear. Think about your lifestyle and how your new clothes will match into your existing wardrobe before buying.

Most brides like to have a new outfit for going-away. Again, choose something which will be a useful addition to your wardrobe, whether it be a suit, a casual outfit or a dress.

The Bridesmaids' Dresses

Choose bridesmaids' dresses which will complement your own dress both in style and colour, and which will suit the girls themselves. As with your own outfit, they must be comfortable to wear as well as beautiful. Don't restrict yourself to bridal shops if you are looking for something different. Shop around in boutiques and department stores.

You can ask the bridesmaids to wear similar dresses, choose a colour and have slightly different styles, or have more than one colour. Most people prefer pastel or subtle shades; anything too strident will not set off your own dress and will look odd in the photographs.

Remember that if your bridesmaids are very different in colouring or age you may need to be more flexible in your approach. A six-year-old will not look good in the same dress as a twenty-year-old, nor a blonde in the same colour as a redhead or a brunette. Even if you choose long dresses for older bridesmaids, it is not a good idea for the younger bridesmaids since they will find them awkward and uncomfortable to wear and may very well trip over them.

The important thing is to maintain the general style, and use similar features in perhaps quite individual dresses to make them complement one another. For example, the older bridesmaids might be wearing peach satin dresses with a fitted bodice, full elbow-length sleeves and a full long skirt trimmed with lace. The child's dress in the same fabric can still be trimmed with lace and have a full sleeve, but the sleeves can be slightly shorter, the skirt to mid-calf, and the bodice be altered to a yoke.

There is no shortage of styles to choose from, from formal dresses in satin and lace to peasant-style dresses with broderie anglaise, Victorian elegance, modern simplicity, or extravagant frills and lace.

Try to imagine the dresses as they will look on each girl. Will it suit them? Can they wear it again? Consider the style of headdress you would like them to wear and whether it will fit with the dress. You can choose hats, headbands or flowers. It is best if they buy their own shoes so that they can make sure of a comfortable fit and have time to wear them in. Ask them to choose a particular style and colour. Find out what their preferences are, how they like to wear their hair, and so on.

Try to bring all the girls together at one time to select or try on the dresses. If you have chosen for them, try to send them a picture so that they feel more involved in the plans.

45

10 Clothes for the Groom and Best Man

THE GROOM, the best man, the ushers and the fathers all dress alike. If the wedding is very formal, you may choose morning suits, and these are usually hired. They are very expensive to buy and this is only economical if you are going to attend formal occasions on a regular basis.

A traditional morning suit is a grey three-piece with a tail coat, or a black tail coat with pinstripe trousers. As a general rule, dark colours are worn for winter and afternoon weddings, lighter colours for summer and morning weddings. You can also hire top hats and gloves for the complete effect, but more often than not these get in the way most of the time! Shoes, socks, shirts and ties (never black) should be bought to match each other. You can ask all the wedding party to wear the same if you prefer, or the groom may elect to be slightly different.

If you are hiring, the outfitter's assistants can advise you of suitable styles, and you can ask the principal men to go along for a fitting.

Make sure they do so well in advance. The suits should fit well and be comfortable, with trousers of the right length.

For a less formal wedding, the principal men may choose two- or three-piece lounge suits. The groom should select his suit first, so that the others can take their cue from him.

Choose colours, for suits and accessories to match the rest of the wedding party. If the bridesmaids are wearing peach, for example, it will look best if the men's suits, ties, handkerchiefs and so on are in a complementary colour.

The same is true of the men's as the girls' outfits: they should look smart and be comfortable. Make sure shoes fit well, have the labels removed and are worn in before the day. Try everything on together and make sure nothing has been forgotten.

Arrange hair cuts a month before the wedding so there is time to rectify any mistakes, if necessary.

11 The Flowers

YOUR WEDDING flowers will complete your outfit, and provide attractive displays both at the church and the reception. Choose flowers that will enhance the mood you want to create and suit the surroundings. Very formal arrangements, for example, would be out of place in a small room or country church.

You will probably want bouquets for the bride and bridesmaids, buttonholes for the principal men and coursages for the bride's and groom's mothers. You may also want flowers at the church or register office. Check with the minister or Superintendent Registrar how this should be arranged. There may be someone at the church who will do the arrangements for you for a small donation. If there are several weddings on the same day, as is very likely, the vicar will be able to give you the names and addresses of the other brides so that you can agree a colour scheme and some flower ideas.

Ideas for your Floral Arrangements

The first thing to do is to decide what you need, whether bouquets, buttonholes and coursages, or whether you also need flowers for the church and reception.

Then think about a basic style and colour scheme – should the flowers be formal or informal, a limited range of colours or a bright, colourful pot pourri?

Look at bridal magazines, florists' catalogues and books about flowers to get an idea of the type of arrangements available. Note what you like and dislike about flowers or arrangements. Do you dislike flowers with large heads? Do you prefer simple or elaborate arrangements? Are there any particular flowers you would like included in the arrangements?

Choosing Colours and Effects

First, think about the colours of the surroundings and of the dresses and choose flowers to suit.

Red, orange and yellow are warm colours which attract attention and are vibrant and lively. Blues and purples are cool colours which create a more restrained atmosphere.

The colours in any arrangement should harmonise and look attractive together. Colours which are too similar to each other will be lacking in effect, whereas opposites may be too strident. The strength of the colour is important, too. A strong, dark colour will overpower a pastel, for example. Picture the sort of effects you want, and try out various colour combinations until you find something which suits the atmosphere you want to create.

Choosing Flowers

If there are particular flowers you would like included, or others that you dislike, then you should let your florist know. Have an idea of some of your favourites as this will help you to choose the style of your flowers. It is best to be guided by the florist on the final choice, since he will know when particular flowers are available, their cost, how long they last and how well they mix with other flowers and with greenery.

The Florist

Select your florist as soon as you can. If you don't know a florist that you want to use, ask other brides, your photographer or friends for suggestions. Visit the florists, if you are not sure, and have a look at their work. You will be able to see the care they take in preparing the flowers, the quality of the blooms and so on. Make sure you like the arrangements. Check that each flower head is carefully arranged and wired. Once you have

chosen the florist, reserve your date as much as four months in advance.

Make an appointment for a planning session six to eight weeks before the wedding date, especially if you want them to prepare the arrangements for the church or reception as well as the bouquets. Go through the catalogue of arrangements and choose those which suit your style, taste and budget. Describe your requirements and preferences, the style of the wedding and the colour and style of the dresses, taking colour swatches if necessary. If there are ribbons and bows in the arrangements, they should be in matching colours.

Be sure to take the florist's advice. Remember that he is an expert on all kinds of flowers – the season that they are readily available, how their colours and shapes blend, their cost and how well they will last in a bouquet or arrangement in a hot room. If you ask for a particular flower which is unsuitable, he will be able to suggest a substitute.

Make sure the florist knows your budget and will work within it. In choosing your arrangements, remember that their cost is mainly determined by the numbers and types of flowers used in them. There is no need to choose out-of-season flowers if the money could be better spent in other ways. Flowers which are readily available will be just as beautiful and cost a great deal less.

Find out the deposit required. This will probably be payable when you order the flowers. The balance may be payable when

the flowers are delivered or beforehand – check this as well. Make sure the florist knows exactly where and when to set up the arrangements, and to deliver the bouquets and buttonholes. As a final check, telephone your florist a few days before the wedding to make sure everything will be ready.

Bouquets and Flowers

The type of wedding you are having will determine the number of flowers you will need and who to buy them for. This list gives you an idea of those you may need to provide flowers for and what you might choose.

Bride

The bride traditionally carries a bouquet which can be white, or a combination of colours of your choice. Make sure it blends with the colours of your bridesmaids' dresses as well as your own. The florist will have a range of styles for you to choose from, ranging from small, round bouquets to large, trailing ones. If you are wearing another colour than white, take a piece of material or a colour match with you when you order the flowers.

Groom, Best Man and Ushers

These wear a buttonhole, usually a white carnation.

Bride's Father and Groom's Father

They also wear a similar buttonhole.

Bride's Mother and Groom's Mother

They usually wear a corsage of orchids or roses. Take along a piece of fabric from each outfit for a proper colour match, or match the outfits to a paint colour selection card and take that.

Bridesmaids

These may carry a bouquet, a nosegay, a basket of flowers or a single flower. The colour and style should match that of the bride. They may also wear a floral wreath or haircomb. Again, colour matching is important. If the bridesmaids are very young, bear in mind that they will get bored holding a bouquet, so a basket will look charming and also be less of a burden, or choose a floral hairband instead.

Arrangements at the Church or Reception

You will probably want several arrangements of flowers at the church. Check what is suitable with the minister, and consult with the other brides concerned if yours is not the only wedding at the church on the day.

For the reception you will almost certainly want a floral centrepiece for the top table. Make sure that it will not block your view of the guests, and their view of you! You may also want arrangements for the cake table, dinner tables or buffet table.

If your budget for the flowers is restricted you could simply have some attractive pots of flowering plants or candles decorated with flowers and greenery, or small arrangements of pretty greenery.

Throwing your Bouquet

It is traditional to throw your bouquet towards the guests when you leave for the honeymoon. The one who catches it is supposed to be the next one to be married! Remember to take a few flowers out of the bouquet to press as a keepsake if you wish.

Saving your Bouquet

If you decide you would rather keep your bouquet, it is possible to have a collage made from the flowers which represents the arrangements of the wedding bouquet. If you like the idea, ask at the local florist or look in Yellow Pages to see if anyone is able to undertake this for you.

12 The Photographs

YOUR SPECIAL day would not be complete without someone recording it on film. Your photograph album will be your permanent record of a wonderful day to look back on with pleasure as the years pass; as they will only too quickly.

You may have offers from friends to take the wedding photographs for you, but it is not generally a good idea since there is no guarantee of the results. Also, if your friend is a guest, you will want them to enjoy the celebration not spend their time behind the camera. Most friends and relations will take their own photographs anyway, so if you want to add some more informal snapshots to your album, it will be easy enough to do so. Most brides agree that it is best to employ a reputable, professional photographer for the occasion.

Choosing the Photographer

Look in the Yellow Pages or in your local high street and you will see that there is a vast choice of wedding photographers. It is up to you to choose the one who will take photographs that you will treasure. See if you can get personal recommendations, and ask to see examples of the photographer's work. The best photographer can make a posed picture look quite natural. The pictures should be clear and sharp and not catch anyone in awkward moments or include backgrounds which detract from the subject of the picture.

Most photographers have a 'wedding package' which will vary from one firm to another. In many cases you pay a standard charge to include his attendance at the wedding to take a certain number of photographs plus one album of about 20 photographs. Make sure you know what you are getting for your money. Don't automatically accept the cheapest quote, go for the best value/quality combination, and a photographer whose style suits your taste. The most expensive, equally, will not necessarily be the best one for you.

When choosing the photographer, these questions may be useful guidelines on what to ask.

1. How long have you been in business?
2. Do you specialise in wedding photography?
3. What packages are available and what are their costs?
4. How much deposit is required and is it refundable under any circumstances?
5. When will the proofs be ready?
6. How long can we retain the proofs?
7. When will the photographs be ready?
8. Is the cost of an album included in the package, or just the photographs?
9. What is the cost of additional albums?
10. What is the cost of additional individual photographs?
11. Do you handle the photograph/ announcement for the press?
12. Are there any extra charges?

Once you have chosen the photographer, meet with him several weeks before the wedding to discuss the package, what kind of pictures you want him to take, and any other arrangements. Most couples find that a mixture of candid and more formal shots are best at capturing every aspect of the day, but you must let the photographer know what you want. There may be a certain time you would prefer that he does not take pictures, you may have seen a particular double-exposure shot you would like, or you may not like very formal poses. Unless you tell the photographer what you want, he cannot take the right pictures. Use the photograph checklist at the back of the book as a guide. Do remember, though, that a good photographer knows his job, and can give you his expert advice on how to get the best album possible. Use his expertise to help you.

Procedure

You will have to pay a deposit when you book the photographer, but do so well in advance so that you have your first choice. You will probably need to specify the package you have chosen, and may want to choose your album at the same time. The bride's and the groom's parents will often decide to have an album as well, or you could consider buying one as a thank-you present for them.

The photographer will take a set number of photographs both before and after the ceremony. Check with the minister or Superintendent Registrar what photographs will be allowed during or after the ceremony. He will then print proofs of all the shots so that you can choose the pictures you would like to buy. Generally, you keep the proofs for a short time, so that you can show them to family and friends in case they want to order any copies. Most photographers do not attend the reception, but you can arrange this if you wish or ask a friend to take some photographs there.

If guests wish to place orders, make sure you know exactly which pictures they want (the proofs will be numbered) and what size. Keep all the information on a list to avoid confusion.

Once you have ordered your photographs, it will usually take a few weeks before they are ready. You will have to pay the final balance before you collect the photographs.

Video

Many brides now decide to have their wedding recorded on video either as well as or instead of photographs. You can either hire a camera or have someone come to take a video, depending on your budget. If you do have a video, you will want to have the tape edited. It isn't likely that you will want to sit through five to six hours of tape every time you want to relive your wedding day.

Keepsake Album

It is surprising how quickly you will forget so many details of your wedding day so it is a good idea to combine your photograph album with a collection of souvenirs of the day. Make a list of the guests, or ask them to sign a guest book during the reception. Note down the names of the wedding party, what they wore and what the flowers were like. Write your impressions of the church, the reception, the flowers, the weather – anything you remember. Press a few flowers from your bouquet, and keep copies of an invitation, an order of service sheet or any other stationery or suitable memento.

13 The Wedding Rings

SYMBOLS HAVE been used throughout history to mark important events in people's lives, such as christenings and weddings. In some ancient cultures, married couples wore a rope of twine around their wrists. Later on, it became customary for the groom to give the bride a present, and eventually this became a ring. This is the custom we retain today. Much more recently, as women's role in society has changed, brides have begun to give a ring to the groom in return. In fact, this now happens in the majority of wedding ceremonies.

There is a vast choice of both engagement and wedding rings from which to choose, so shop around before actually going out to buy the rings. The more you know about what is available, the better your chances of making a good selection. It is a good idea to shop together so that you are sure your fiancé is happy with your choice. Remember, that ring will be worn constantly for years, so you want it to be right.

Most jewellers stock a good choice of rings to suit every price range. It is a good idea to tell him how much you want to spend before you start, so that you will not be tempted to buy a ring that you cannot really afford. Naturally the rings you and your husband will wear are very important to you, but you will be needing many practical items too, and a less expensive ring will symbolise your commitment just as well.

If you need to arrange additional finance, do so before you shop. Otherwise you may choose a ring which is really out of your range, and later regret that you obtained a loan which is difficult to repay.

Most people choose from the range offered by the jeweller, but you may be fortunate enough to be able to choose an individual ring, in which case the following information will be particularly useful in helping you to make the best choice.

Don't forget also, that you could choose an antique ring which may perhaps be less expensive although equally beautiful and durable, but do buy from a reputable and expert dealer.

The Jeweller

Always choose a reputable jeweller. Either ask friends or relatives for a recommendation, or go to a high street jeweller whose name you respect. Don't be tempted to deal with anyone whose reputation is dubious. It is very difficult for anyone but an expert to value jewellery, and unless you are professional yourself, you need to rely on the jeweller's skill. You can, if you wish, obtain an independent valuation.

You may wish to find out the store's policy with regard to return, exchange, refund, repair or replacement. If there is a guarantee, make sure it indicates what it does and does not cover and who will honour it. It is helpful if the receipt includes details of the ring: materials of which it is composed; gem quality; carat weight; as well as the price, in case this is required for insurance purposes.

If you have entered into a credit agreement of some kind to buy the ring, make sure you know exactly how much interest you will pay, when the payments are due and when the balance is due. Clearly understand what happens if your are late with a payment. Find out about warranties and insurance cover until it is paid for.

Diamonds

Diamonds are the most popular stones for an engagement ring. The choice of settings is practically infinite, and includes everything from a single stone, a solitaire, to arrangements of diamonds, or diamonds combined with other stones.

The actual shape of the diamond is known as the cut, and the artistry of the cutter is in creating a stone with maximum sparkle. Not all rough diamonds can be cut into any shape, hence the fact that some stones are more expensive than others of the same carat weight.

The most perfect diamonds are clear and colourless, with the faintest hint of blue.

Magnified ten times, a perfect diamond

shows no flaws, and this is known as perfect clarity. Of course, a minutely flawed stone can still be exceptionally beautiful.

There are particular specialist terms used to define the quality of a diamond, such as 'royal' or 'radiant', although you do not need to be familiar with these when buying an engagement ring. If the jeweller uses a term you do not understand, simply ask him to explain.

The carat weight of a diamond is the measure of its size. The larger the stone the higher the carat weight. Large stones are obviously the most expensive because they are rare, although the best stones are judged not only by weight but also by cut, colour, clarity and quality, so the largest stone may not necessarily be the best one.

You may choose not to have a diamond engagement ring, or you may want to have a diamond combined with other stones. Some brides have a particular favourite, want a coloured stone, or like to choose their own birthstone.

Birthstones

Some people like to choose their birthstone for their engagement ring. Each stone is associated with a particular month and to symbolise a particular quality in the person.

January	Garnet (dark red)	Constancy
February	Amethyst (purple)	Sincerity
March	Bloodstone (green with red flecks)	Courage
April	Diamond	Innocence
May	Emerald (green)	Success
June	Pearl (white or pink)	Purity
July	Ruby (red)	Love and contentment
August	Sardonyx (white with yellow or orange-red)	Married bliss
September	Sapphire (blue)	Wisdom
October	Opal (white, red or turquoise with coloured flecks)	Hope
November	Topaz (brown, pink or yellow)	Fidelity
December	Turquoise (turquoise)	Harmony

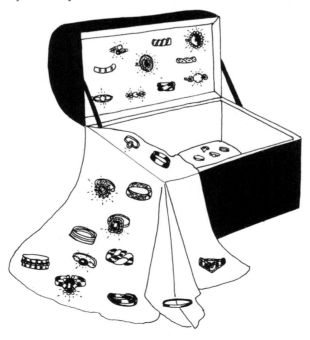

Choosing Gemstones

If you hold a diamond under a concentrated light, it should sparkle with as white a colour as possible when held at all angles. If you examine a coloured stone in the light, it should be intense, lively and clear, but not to the point that you can see through it.

It is not true that only a real diamond can cut glass. Many things, including glass, will cut glass.

When examining gems, remember that the cut is important to their value. Sometimes they may be poorly cut to maintain weight, at the expense of quality.

The Setting

If you are choosing a setting select one that will beautifully set off your stone. Remember that the size of your hand and fingers should also influence your choice. A wide, heavy band would suit large hands, but overwhelm small ones.

Wedding Rings

Wedding rings are usually plain bands, most commonly of yellow or white gold. They might be flat, rounded, carved or plain. Choose one to complement your engagement ring as most people like to wear them together.

If you decide to have your rings engraved, perhaps with your initials and wedding date, remember to allow four to six weeks for this to be done. The longer the time you allow the better – just in case it takes longer than anticipated.

Metals

Gold is the most popular metal for engagement and wedding rings, and it is usually yellow gold, although white gold is also popular. The amount of gold is measured in carats, with pure gold being 24 carats. However, pure gold is too soft for jewellery, so it is alloyed with other metals. A 14 carat gold ring would be 14 parts gold mixed with 10 parts of another metal. Most wedding rings are between 14 carats and 18 carats.

The ring should have a hallmark confirming its quality.

Platinum is a beautiful choice for wedding rings and is extremely durable. It is, however, more expensive than gold.

Insurance

You should insure your rings against loss, theft or damage (loss of a stone, for example). Most insurance companies will require a certificate of its value from a jeweller. Rings can usually be added to your household insurance, but should be listed separately as items of particular value and ones which are to be insured at all times, not just when they are in the house. If you are not sure of your cover, ask your insurance company or agent.

Cleaning

Check now and then for loose stones and have your ring professionally cleaned every few years. Every month or so clean the rings yourself. Pearls, opals and turquoise should be cleaned with a dry cloth. For others, soak in hot water and detergent, scrub with a toothbrush, rinse and dry.

Remember to remove your rings when doing housework or cleaning the car. It is not good for the rings, and you will not be too happy if the diamonds scratch the finishes!

14 The Wedding Cake

THE WEDDING cake is one of the focal points of the reception. Many styles are available, but these ideas may help you to make your decision.

You may order your cake from a bakery, from your caterer, or you may have a talented friend or relation who will make and decorate it for you. Many people run home businesses making wedding cakes, and they may be excellent and very reasonably priced. Ask other brides or friends or look in Yellow Pages. Before making a decision, visit several suppliers and look at their sample books and pictures, ask their prices, and taste their products before your order!

Order at least two months before your wedding to make sure the baker has time to make the cake.

The size of the cake is up to you, but the baker will be able to advise you what size you will need for the number of guests you are

having. Remember also that you may want to send some small pieces to people who cannot attend the reception. Some people also like to save the top tier for a christening! As a general rule, a 25-cm tier will serve up to 18 people, a 30-cm round cake will serve 24-36 people, depending on the size of the pieces.

You can choose the shape of the cake, but the most popular are square or round. You can have a single cake, or several tiers separated by pillars. Traditionally, a wedding cake is a rich fruit cake with white royal icing piped and decorated. The supplier will offer a selection of designs and decorations. Most people like to have a special decoration on the top, perhaps a vase of fresh flowers or a bride and groom decoration. You may be able to buy or rent this from the baker, or you may wish to buy one elsewhere.

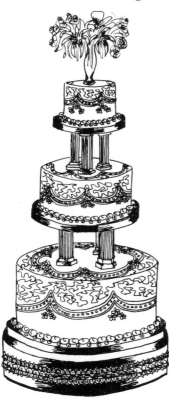

15 Transport

MOST PEOPLE like a special car for their wedding day, and you may choose to hire a Rolls-Royce, or even an antique car or a horse-drawn carriage. If you do choose an open carriage, don't forget that the weather is unpredictable. This can be expensive, but does add a little flair to the day. Usually, people hire this one special car to take the bride and her father to the ceremony, and the bride and groom to the reception. In most cases, these cars are chauffeur-driven.

Book as early as possible. Make sure you know the full cost, any deposit required, the car the hire company will provide, and the substitute car they will send should anything go wrong. Find out if the chauffeur is provided, whether he will be in uniform, the insurance cover and whether there are any extra charges. If you choose a reputable firm, they will probably have a wedding package which will make everything quite clear. You should make sure they know the venues, dates and times they are required.

If you would rather not spend a great deal on transport, you can ask around to see if a friend or relation has a smart car you could borrow for the day: scarlet, silver or maroon, or perhaps something to tie in with the overall colour scheme, would all be very stylish. Perhaps your own car would fit the bill; try it out with some wedding ribbons and a few flowers – fresh, dried or silk – in the back window and you will probably be pleasantly surprised.

If you hire a car, the hire company will provide the traditional white ribbons, otherwise you may want to buy these. You may also want to put ribbons on the cars to carry the bridesmaids or others in the wedding party.

You will also need to make arrangements for the bridesmaids and the bride's mother to arrive at the ceremony, and for them and the bride's father and groom's parents to be driven to the reception. The best man is responsible for getting the groom to the church and the bride and groom to the reception, and should take charge of the arrangements for getting the other guests safely dispatched to the reception. You can hire cars if necessary, or arrange for the ushers to chauffeur the bridesmaids, and friends or relatives to provide transport for others who do not have their own. There are no rules, as long as everyone is transported safely and no one is left behind.

If you are asking friends to help out, offer to pay for petrol and a car wash. Have a few back-up cars and drivers available just in case. Make sure everyone knows in advance who they will transport (or who will transport them), and provide maps if necessary.

The best man should make sure that the groom's car is safely parked at the reception site ready for the couple to leave on their honeymoon. It is fun for some of the guests to decorate the car, but have a word with the best man to make sure they don't go too far and use anything which might damage the paintwork. If you have a plane to catch, remember to allow time to stop and tidy up the car, and have some spare cloths and rubbish bags in the boot!

16 Wedding Gifts

IT IS traditional for people attending the wedding to give a gift to the couple, and you will probably receive other wedding gifts as well. The choice of gift is obviously up to the guest, but everyone wants their gift to be well received, so most people like to consult the couple before buying.

Wedding Present List

It is a good idea to draw up a wedding present list for people to consult if they wish. Traditional wedding presents usually include mainly items for the new home, but there is no reason why you should stick to this if you prefer to include some more personal items.

Always include a range of things on the list, from inexpensive to more expensive. Don't be afraid to include a few choices on your list that are relatively expensive, since some people might like to club together to buy a single present. Also include more items than you expect to receive. Otherwise the last people to receive the list will have little choice.

Usually, the bride keeps the list and sends it to anyone who requests it. They tick off the item they would like to buy and return it to the bride.

Some department stores will organise the list for you. You visit the store and choose items that you would like to have in your new home. You can indicate colours and patterns that you like, and fill out a form for the things you select. When friends and family select a gift from the list, they eliminate it to avoid duplication. Stores who offer mail order can also serve customers who live at a distance.

Thank You Letters

Always make a note of presents as you receive them and write thank you letters as you go along. That way, you can enjoy writing a personal note, rather than being faced with a whole list of letters to write.

You can buy printed thank-you cards, but these are rather impersonal.

Presents at the Reception

Hopefully you will receive most presents before the reception, but many people will bring presents with them. Have a table handy behind the receiving line to avoid juggling parcels while you are trying to greet guests. Perhaps some of the younger bridesmaids could help. If it is at all possible, try to find the time at least to glance at the presents so you can make some personal thank yous; again younger helpers can usually be found, particularly to make sure that labels are stuck to the right present.

Displaying the Presents

It is customary to display the wedding presents in the bride's home. It is best to arrange them in a spare room or dining room, rather than your main living area, and each gift should have a card to say from whom it was received. It is better to display them in a private house, even if this means arranging for people to come and see them, since you may encourage uninvited guests if you display at a hotel or reception venue, and you are advertising the contents of your new home. You can have the display on the wedding day or beforehand if most of your guests are local.

Arrange your gifts in groups, so that all the linen is together, all the glass and so on. But if you have received two very similar or even identical items it will be most tactful to separate them. You should also avoid embarrassing anyone by placing an inexpensive present next to an extravagant one, and you should never reveal the amount of any gift of money. If you receive a dinner service or sets of linen, it is quite proper to display only one place setting or one sheet and pillow case.

Don't show any gifts which may have been damaged in the post unless they can be arranged to hide the damage.

You should bear in mind the value of your gifts when arranging household contents insurance, and perhaps consider temporary cover if you are going to display them at the reception.

Returns and Exchanges

You must of course never tell anyone their present was not what you wanted. Some shops will allow you to exchange an item, but even if you have simply got a different colour it would not be tactful to reveal this in your thank-you note.

In the unfortunate event of a gift arriving damaged, you should first find out whether it was insured by either the shop or the carrier. If at all possible it is better not to tell the giver, since they may feel obliged to buy a replacement.

17 Pre-Wedding Parties

MOST BRIDES like to have a hen party a week or so before the wedding to enjoy an evening out with their bridesmaids and friends. You can choose a meal in a smart restaurant, or any way you wish to relax among friends and to say thank you for their help. Some brides choose to give the bridesmaids' presents at the party, or you can keep them until the day and give them before you leave for the church.

Try to persuade your groom to hold his stag party the week before the wedding rather than the night before! The best man usually organises this, and again a group of the groom's closest friends go out and enjoy themselves for a meal and usually a few drinks. It is up to the best man to make sure that the groom – and the other guests – get home safely, so he should either abstain himself, or perhaps arrange for a taxi or other suitable transport home for the revellers.

Some people like to hold a small dinner party for their family, the wedding party and their partners after the rehearsal at the church. It is a nice way to thank family and friends for their support.

18 The Rehearsal

A REHEARSAL is often held the week before the wedding so that the wedding party can have a final check on their roles, where they should be and what they should be doing. Most people find it a useful way of ironing out any last-minute worries and re-assuring everyone that things will go well on the day. Not all ministers feel that it is necessary.

The minister will probably run through the ceremony and point out where each person should be during the service. You can take the opportunity to check all the details and make sure everything will go smoothly on the day.

Go through their duties with the chief bridesmaid and the best man. Make a list of the things they should remember if you think it will help, and give the best man a note of anyone he should particularly mention in his speech.

It makes a pleasant event to hold a dinner for the wedding party after the rehearsal, or to go out for a meal or a small celebration with those closest to you. It gives you and the groom a chance to show your appreciation for the hard work others will be putting into your special day.

19 The Ceremony

THIS IS the most essential part of your wedding day: the ceremony itself. This chapter will touch on all aspects of the ceremony, from setting the time and place and making the bookings, to what actually happens on the day.

The Date

There are a number of things to consider when you are deciding on the date of your wedding. Many brides favour a particular season, but particularly if you are having a large or formal wedding it is very important to allow enough time for the preparations. You will also have to consider the convenience of your guests and avoid times when many are likely to be on holiday, or when the weather may make travel difficult.

When you have decided roughly when your wedding will be, you must find out the dates on which the church will be available. Some religious denominations forbid marriages on certain days or at certain times, and the minister will of course tell you if this is the case. Many weddings take place on Saturdays, and this will certainly be easier for all your guests who are working. However, it is quite acceptable to have a week-day wedding if this suits those concerned.

The Place

If you want a civil ceremony, you should go to see the local Superintendent Registrar as early as possible. Find out about all the legal formalities of residence qualifications and obtaining a licence. Check how many guests can be accommodated at the ceremony and whether photographs can be taken in the register office.

If you wish to be married in a church, then you should talk first to the minister. He will discuss your plans with you and book the date and time of the wedding. You will probably be asked to attend several meetings either with him or with a member of the church to go through the ceremony and discuss the implications of the commitment you are making to each other. You may be able to choose whether to follow the traditional service, or the more popular modern form. You will be expected to attend services together.

It is traditional to choose the bride's church, although the groom's church is often used. If you wish to marry in a different church, then you must consult with the minister.

If you are of different faiths, you should discuss your feelings openly with one another and choose a church you are both happy with. If you are Church of England and the groom is a Catholic, for example, you may wish to be married in your church and arrange for your future husband's priest to attend and give you his blessing.

Arranging the Details

As well as discussing the ceremony itself, you should find out about other aspects of the service. Can you arrange for the choir or a soloist? Will the photographer be allowed to take photographs in the church? What music will be played and can you choose the music for entering and leaving the church and while you are signing the register? Can you arrange for bell ringing? Ask if your guests will be allowed to throw confetti in the church grounds and whether you can choose your own hymns. If you want to arrange for Order of Service sheets, you should check all the details with the minister to avoid any confusion. Find out about flowers for the church, and if there are to be other weddings on the same day, ask for the names and addresses of the other brides so that you can agree on the floral arrangements.

If yours is to be a civil ceremony, there will still be many of these arrangements to check, although the ceremony is likely to be simpler.

Music

Your choice of music will help to create the atmosphere, whether it is something traditional or a favourite piece, but make sure you agree the choice with the minister, and that it can be played on the church organ. If not, you can arrange a tape.

Some ideas for processional music include: The Bridal March (Wagner); Grand March (Verdi); Processional March (Handel); Wedding Processional (Harris).

While you are signing the register, you may have music, or the choir or a soloist may sing. Ave Maria (Schubert) or Jesus, Joy of Man's Desiring (Bach) are popular.

The recessional music is celebratory, such as Mendelssohn's Wedding March.

Church of England Weddings

The guests begin to arrive about 20 minutes before the service while the organist plays quietly. The ushers are responsible for escorting guests to their seats. The front pews are reserved for close family, with bride's relations and friends on the left hand side of the church, and the groom's relations and friends on the right hand side. If one family is much larger, you can ask the ushers to show mutual friends to seats on the other side so that everyone has the best view.

The groom and best man should arrive in good time so they can pose for a few photographs and pay the fees to the minister. They then sit in the front pew on the right hand side. The bride's mother arrives with the bridesmaids, and waits in the church porch until the bride and her father arrive before taking her place. The head usher should escort her to her pew.

The bride is normally escorted by her father, but if he is deceased or unable to attend, you can be escorted by your step-father, brother, friend, or any male relative.

When the bride and her father are ready at the church entrance, the organist will play the entrance music, and the congregation stand. The bride walks up the aisle on her father's right arm, followed by the bridesmaids. If it is a full choral service, the minister may meet the bride in the porch and the procession will be led by the choir, followed by the minister, the bride and her father and the bridesmaids. Often, the minister will greet the bride in the porch, then return to the altar before the procession.

As the bride reaches the chancel steps, the groom gets his first look at her in her bridal

Places During the Ceremony

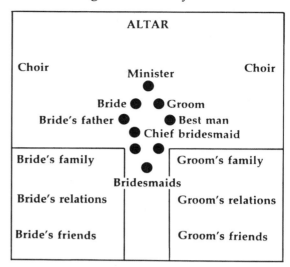

gown. Tell the groom to take a good look and imprint that picture on his memory. Then he can recall that wonderful moment later – in the middle of a row, perhaps – to good effect! At the chancel steps, the bride stands on the groom's left. Her father stands to her left and a pace behind her. The best man stands on the groom's right, and again slightly behind him. The chief bridesmaid takes the bride's bouquet. If there are no bridesmaids, the bride's father normally takes the bouquet and hands it to his wife to hold until later.

The ceremony then begins. The minister explains the significance of marriage and calls on the bride, groom and congregation to declare if there is any reason why the couple may not lawfully marry. He then asks the bride and groom in turn whether they promise to love, comfort, honour and protect the other, forsaking all others 'as long as you both shall live'. They reply, 'I will'.

The groom takes the bride's right hand in his and they exchange vows. The best man gives the ring to the minister, and the groom places it on the bride's left hand. If the couple are exchanging rings, the bride also places her ring on the groom's hand. The groom gives the ring as a sign of their marriage and makes his promise to the bride to love, honour and share everything with her. The bride responds with the same promise and the minister pronounces them man and wife.

The minister usually gives a short address before the signing of the register, and the wedding party will sit down in the front pews during this. There may also be hymns, prayers or singing. Then it is time to go to the vestry to sign the register. The minister is followed by the bride and groom, the best man and the chief bridesmaid, followed by the bridesmaids. The groom's father takes the arm of the bride's mother, and the bride's father takes the arm of the groom's mother. The ladies take the left arms of their escorts. The best man and the chief bridesmaid often act as the two witnesses, but you may prefer to ask your parents. One or two photographs are usually taken in the vestry.

The bride then takes her bouquet from the chief bridesmaid and the wedding party leave the church to the recessional music: the bride on the left arm of her husband; followed by the chief bridesmaid and the best man; the bride's mother and the groom's father; the groom's mother and the bride's father; the bridesmaids, often escorted by the ushers. Relatives leave next and are followed by friends. The church bells ring out. Some couples emerge to a guard of honour in keeping with their jobs or hobbies: a ceremonial party for a military couple; schoolchildren for teachers and so on.

Outside, everyone can really relax, and the photographs are usually taken. The bride and groom are usually the first to leave for the reception, and the guests throw confetti (if it is allowed) or rice as they leave.

Roman Catholic Weddings

As with all marriages outside the Church of England, the couple must give notice of their intention to marry to the local Superintendent Registrar as detailed in the chapter on The Legal Requirements. Usually the priest is authorised to register the marriage, otherwise a registrar will need to be present.

Where both the couple are Catholic, the ceremony usually takes place at a Nuptual Mass, although it can be conducted outside Mass, and this is most likely if one of the couple is not a Roman Catholic.

The ceremony itself is very similar in content to the Church of England ceremony. The priest addresses the bride and groom on the significance of marriage within the Church. The couple must declare that there is no lawful reason why they may not be married;

they promise to be faithful to each other and to accept and bring up children within the Roman Catholic faith. The priest invites them to declare their consent to marry according to the rites of the Church, to which they reply, 'I will'. The couple join right hands and call upon the congregation to witness the marriage. They then make their vows to cherish one another 'Till death do us part'. The priest confirms them in marriage and the rings are blessed and given or exchanged, with the couple acknowledging them as a token of their love and fidelity.

Jewish Weddings

Notice to marry must be given to the Superintendent Registrar, but a Jewish wedding may take place in a synagogue or a private house. Wherever the ceremony is held, the secretary of the groom's synagogue must take down the necessary particulars.

The ceremony itself can vary, depending on the synagogue. At the United Synagogue, they use a very ancient form of service. The bride and groom stand under a chuppah, a canopy, which is a reminder of when the Israelites were forced to live in tents and symbolises the importance of the couple's new home together. The couple's parents may also stand under the chuppah, and the relations and friends stand behind. Next to the rabbi is a small covered table with two cups of ritual wine and one glass wrapped in a white napkin.

The rabbi delivers a short address to the couple and then the groom says to the bride, 'Behold, thou art consecrated unto me by this ring, according to the law of Moses and Israel'. He gives her a ring. They then read and sign the Hebrew marriage contract. They both promise to be true and faithful, to love, honour and cherish each other. The groom also promises to support the bride.

They take their vows and the rabbi recites the Seven Benedictions. They each take a sip of wine from the glass, twice over, then the groom smashes the glass on the ground. This is a reminder that they should share each other's pleasures and halve each other's troubles. The broken glass symbolises the weakness of marriage without love. They then sign a covenant of marriage detailing their promises to each other.

20 The Reception

WHEN THE ceremony is over and you are husband and wife at last, you will be able to really relax and enjoy yourself with your guests. It is very much up to you whether you choose to have a formal 'wedding breakfast', a buffet, or a small dinner for close relations and friends and perhaps a party in the evening. The numbers involved and your budget will be the most important factors in determining your choice. Whatever you choose, the reception is the culmination of your wedding day when you can share your happiness with others.

In any case, the first things to finalise are the size of your guest list, the amount of money you will spend and the type of reception it will be. You can then go about choosing a venue. The following notes will give you some ideas to think about when making your choice.

Choosing the Venue

The number of guests and the budget are obviously vital factors. Do not be swayed into spending more than you originally intended. A reception can be an expensive affair, but it can be just as enjoyable on a smaller scale. If you are constantly worrying about how much it is costing, you are not going to enjoy yourselves.

You can hold the reception at the bride's parents' home, or any other suitable house. This makes for a pleasant and informal atmosphere, but you do need a sufficiently large house to avoid a squash. Outside caterers are still a good idea otherwise the bride's mother, in particular, will be far too busy to enjoy the day. You will also need crockery, cutlery and so on, which the caterer would be able to supply.

Hotels and clubs often have rooms which they hire out for wedding receptions. The hotel may supply the food, catering staff and so on, or you can make your own arrangements.

You could also choose a church or village hall, and invite outside caterers. Make sure that the church allows the consumption of alcohol on the premises, if you wish to supply more than soft drinks for your wedding guests.

If you hire a room, find out about any rules and regulations you must follow, and have a contact number for information or emergencies. It is a good idea to have a written agreement for the booking, including all the details provided. Make sure there is ample parking, heating is sufficient (for a winter wedding), chairs and tables are provided and so on. Even if you are having a buffet, you will need plenty of space and chairs so people can relax. If there are children you may need highchairs. You should book as far in advance as possible, six months is ideal, then confirm the booking nearer the time.

You may want to arrange for the room to be decorated with flowers, paper flowers, balloons or streamers to add to the joyful atmosphere.

The Receiving Line

At a formal or semi-formal reception, there is usually a receiving line at the door to welcome the guests. It is a good idea to go over the guest list with both parents the day before the wedding so that everyone's names are fresh in your mind.

The traditional order of the receiving line is: the bride's mother and father, the groom's mother and father, and the bride and groom. Greet each guest by name, and if you don't know, smile and ask. Don't panic if you can't remember everyone – no one will expect you to. You and the groom should introduce each other to guests when necessary. They will express their best wishes to the bride and congratulations to the groom. Welcome them briefly and let them continue down the line. This is not the moment to catch up on news!

You should offer the guests a glass of wine or an aperitif as they reach the end of the line, and the best man, chief bridesmaid and ushers can help to introduce people to each other and make sure they feel welcome. You may like the guests to sign a register. When all the guests have been welcomed, you can start to take your places at the tables, and the guests will follow suit.

Seating at the Reception

For a formal reception, there will usually be a top table for the wedding party, then other tables as required. The top table is reserved for the wedding party. Be careful not to hurt anyone's feelings by including a guest who is not a member of the wedding party, although you can include younger bridesmaids or partners of the wedding party if you wish and if there is room.

It is a good idea to work out a seating plan before the reception, with the hotel manager or caterer if you wish, and to place seating cards so that everyone can find their place. Remember to do so in a way that enables each person to be near someone they know, yet have an opportunity to meet new people. Alternate men and women every other chair. A husband and wife are usually seated at the same table, but not necessarily next to each other. Make sure you separate any guests you know don't get on with each other. You may wish to place a large seating chart near the door so that it is easier for the guests to find their seat.

Seating at the Top Table

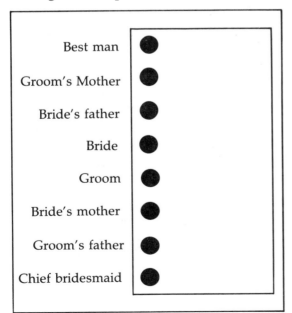

Best man	●
Groom's Mother	●
Bride's father	●
Bride	●
Groom	●
Bride's mother	●
Groom's father	●
Chief bridesmaid	●

The Wedding Breakfast

What you choose for the wedding breakfast will be determined by cost and numbers. Discuss it well in advance with the caterer, who will probably offer a selection of packages. If in doubt, ask their advice, since they should be experienced at what makes for a successful meal.

If you choose a buffet meal, you may like to ask everyone to find their seats, then rise a table at a time to go and get their meal, starting with the top table. The caterers will help with this.

However you are arranging the meal, make sure you remember all the details, not just the food. Cutlery and crockery are obvious essentials, but you should also have serving cutlery, serviettes, possibly smaller cutlery or extra spoons for children, and so on. If it is a buffet meal, allow some additional cutlery if possible, since someone always leaves their fork on a table and takes another.

Remember that the caterers are the experts, so don't be afraid to ask their advice.

The Speeches and Toasts

The speeches, toasts and cake-cutting ceremony usually take place after the last course. The first to speak is the bride's father who stands and says a few words about the bride and groom, before proposing the main toast to them. The groom then responds, usually saying how fortunate he is to have such a lovely wife, thanking the bride's parents and his own for a wonderful wedding, and the guests for their presents. He may thank anyone else who has been particularly helpful, such as the relation who made the cake, for example. He acknowledges the services of the best man and proposes a toast to the bridesmaids. The best man replies for the bridesmaids, thanking the groom and adding a few compliments of his own. He may have a few anecdotes about the couple, as long as they are not embarrassing, or some well-kept secrets from the groom's past which will amuse the guests. He congratulates the bride and groom and reads the congratulatory telegrams.

Make sure the groom and the best man know who to single out for particular thanks;

you can write them a short list, but don't make it too long or involved. The best speeches are informal, short and to-the-point, since most people are not professional speech-makers and it can be nerve-wracking to stand up in front of a large group of people. If you think you can amuse the guests with a humorous anecdote or an inoffensive joke, then by all means include it, but if you doubt your abilities, it is best to keep it simple and sincere. Speak slowly and clearly but don't shout. Practise your speech aloud so that you are sure it is easy to deliver.

More often today, the bride chooses to say a few words herself, and when you decide to fit this into the speeches is really up to you, since it is a relatively recent addition! It usually fits in after the best man. You may want to say your own thank-yous, in which case make sure everyone knows roughly what you intend to say, rather than overlapping with other speeches. Every speech needs on-the-spot alterations to make it work well, but try to keep these to a minimum.

Cutting the Cake

The cake is usually placed on the top table, although not in such a way as to block everyone's view of the happy couple. After the speeches, the best man will announce that the bride and groom will cut the cake. Make sure you have a really sharp, suitable cake knife, since iced wedding cakes can be hard to cut. You may want to have it cut through beforehand. Hold the knife in your right hand, with the groom's right hand on yours, and your left hand on top, and cut the first slice together. The cake can then be moved so that it can be cut for the guests, or it can be the signal to leave the tables to mingle with your guests. Some brides like to send pieces of cake in cake boxes to friends who cannot attend the wedding, or save the top tier for a christening.

Dancing

You will already have made arrangements for musicians, a discotheque, or taped music at the reception to suit your taste. Refer to the chapter on Entertainment for more information.

Traditionally, the bride and groom start the dancing with a slow dance. Then the best man and the chief bridesmaid join in, followed by the two sets of parents, then the other guests. Some time during the evening you should dance with all the members of your wedding party of the opposite sex, and your immediate family members. Try to make sure that no one is left out, and remind the groom and best man to circulate with as many dancing partners as possible.

Leave Taking

At some stage during the reception, slip away with the chief bridesmaid to change into your going-away outfit. You should have this ready in a separate room somewhere convenient. The groom may also wish to change. Try to find a moment for a quiet word with your parents and others who have contributed a lot to the wedding to thank them for a wonderful day.

You may wish to have an informal leave-taking line. The guests line up with the men on one side and the ladies on the other. The groom goes down one side, thanking the ladies for coming to the wedding and kissing them goodbye. You move down the other line. The wedding party and your parents should be the last in line. Then everyone goes outside so the guests can give you a final send-off to your honeymoon. The bride usually throws her bouquet towards the guests before leaving.

21 Food and Drink

FOOD AND drink are usually served at the celebrations after a wedding ceremony, but what type of meal you offer is up to you. Some couples select a ceremony time that will allow them to serve a luncheon buffet, others prefer a more formal meal or cocktails and hors d'oeuvres. The only rules are those of common sense. Don't expect either yourself or your guests to enjoy a three-hour midday party without lunch, or serve the meal too early in the reception if people will have just eaten before they arrived. There may also be local or ethnic traditions you wish to follow.

Preparing your own Food

If you decide to prepare and serve the food yourself, a buffet is the simplest answer as you can do as much as possible of the preparation in advance. But don't underestimate the amount of work involved, and remember that all the food has to be displayed, then cleared away.

Choose a menu that is already familiar to you and select items that are not difficult or complicated to make. Prepare and freeze as much as possible in advance so that you can concentrate on the fresh foods the day before or the morning of the wedding. Don't forget that it takes much longer to prepare food in large quantities. It is easier to prepare reasonable-size batches than trying to make very large quantities of one dish at the same time. Avoid too large a choice of dishes if you are not sure you will have time for the preparation.

Your recipes will specify the number of servings, but the size of the servings will vary, and not every guest will choose every dish, so try to work out quantities carefully so that there is enough, but not too much left over. If you have a choice of three cold meats, for example, assume that most people will have one slice of each of two meats when determining quantities. Caterers generally allow about 15 items per person for a buffet.

Catering

Most people prefer to hire a caterer since they do all the work for you of providing the food, crockery and cutlery, serving where necessary, and clearing up. For a larger wedding, this allows the bride and her mother, in particular, to concentrate on enjoying the reception. It is also much nicer for your parents if they don't have to do the cleaning after an exhausting day.

Take care in choosing a caterer who will suit your needs. Ask around for recommendations, look at their brochures and ask about the service they offer. See and taste the food if you can. Most caterers will have a choice of menus for wedding meals or buffets from which you can choose depending on budget, numbers of guests and what style of meal you prefer.

If you choose a sit-down meal, it is best not to be too adventurous since everyone will have to eat the same. For example, a very spicy main course may not be popular. A selection of vegetables is also a good idea, but concentrate on the most popular varieties rather than serving something very unusual. Remember that colour and presentation are important, too. Don't serve chicken with cauliflower and boiled potatoes; go for green beans and carrots to add colour.

A finger buffet or fork buffet allow guests a little more scope in choosing what they like, so go for a range of tastes and include both popular and unusual.

If you have invited children, make sure there are things they will like, and take account of any vegetarians, or anyone with other special dietary requirements.

Most caterers charge a flat fee based on the number of guests attending and the menu you choose. Find out whether this includes service, clearing up, crockery, cutlery, napkins and so on.

Make sure the caterer has all the necessary details of the venue, the time they should be setting up, the time the wedding party is expected and when you would like them to serve the meal.

Food Ideas

The caterers will offer you selected menus so that you can choose your food for a sit-down meal or a buffet, or you can spend time going through recipe books to choose what you want. Here are a few ideas of things to be thinking about when you are selecting the food.

Starters should whet your appetite for the main course to follow, so especially for a luncheon, choose something light and delicate. A simple hors d'oeuvre, a prawn dish or a melon or grapefruit dish are good ideas. For a winter luncheon, a delicious simple soup is a good warming alternative.

Your main course should not be too spicy, should be easy to eat, and likely to please most of the guests. Roast meats are a good choice, served with a suitable gravy or sauce, or perhaps braised cutlets or a chicken pie. For a summer wedding, you might choose a salad meal. Select your vegetables to complement the main dish both in taste and presentation.

Most people choose a cold dessert since you will not be able to tell exactly when the dessert will be served if everyone is busy chatting to friends and relations while they eat. If you have chosen a rich main course, go for something light and refreshing; a sorbet, fruit salad or mousse. To follow a lighter main course, you may want a gateau, fruit tart or pie.

For a buffet meal, start thinking about basics first: bread, meats and cheeses, quiches, sandwiches or rolls. Then add a selection of salads with dressings, and smaller items such as crudités and dips, cottage cheese and celery boats, tiny meatballs, sausage rolls, crisps and nuts. Finally make a dessert selection. Always bear in mind how the food is to be eaten: with fingers, forks or a knife and fork, since this can make quite a difference to your choice.

Drinks

You will naturally want to provide liquid refreshment for your guests. The caterer may be able to supply a glass a sherry for each guest as they arrive, wine with the meal, and Champagne for the toasts. Check their prices, exactly what they are providing, and whether glasses are included.

For the remainder of the reception, there may be a bar available at the hotel or reception venue with a bartender provided. You can then either leave your guests to purchase their own drinks, pay the full bar bill yourselves, or give a certain amount of money to the barman. Once this is exhausted, guests then pay for their own drinks.

If you supply your own drinks, the type and quantities you will need will depend on your guests. Try to have a reasonable range, including a good quantity of mixers and soft drinks both for the children and the drivers. Ask the caterer or hotel manager for advice, or ask other brides. A bottle of wine or Champagne will yield about eight glasses, a litre of spirits will serve about 16. You can buy a barrel of beer, but remember that it must all be drunk, so don't buy too much. It may be suitable to buy one barrel and supplement it with cans.

It is better to have someone who will act as barman, or a number of people who will help out. You will not want the groom or the best man to spend the reception behind the bar when they should be enjoying the reception with the guests. If you hire a barman, check references or go on personal recommendation and make sure you know how much you are paying before the event.

22 Entertainment at the Reception

THE STYLE of music you choose for your reception depends on what you and your guests like. Try to have music that will allow everyone to be happy and have a good time. Although it is true that it is your reception, you invited the guests to celebrate with you, so make it easy for them to do so. Look through the guest list and try to make sure that everyone is catered for. You may find the ages range from one to seventy so there will be plenty of variety.

Besides ensuring that it is acceptable to all your guests, you can use the music to set the tone for the style of reception you want. If you want everyone to dance, you must provide plenty of dance music; if you are planning a quieter reception then sophisticated background music would be a better choice. Most people opt for a mixture of the two, or assume that guests will want to talk first and start dancing later on.

Musicians

If you want live music, choose a band that can play a little of everything: a waltz, some rock music, gentle songs interspersed with lively dances. Make sure the band you choose can provide this variety and sound the way you want them to. Let the band know the kind of music you want and how often you want it played. For example, you might ask them to play two or three slow dances, followed by a 60s song, then a few rock songs. If you have any special songs you want played, tell them in time to make sure they can learn them before the wedding if necessary. Choose the first dance, too, as you and the groom will dance to that alone. Let them know whether you would like dances like the Hokey Cokey, the Conga and so on, and what tunes you would like for the last dance or at particular moments during the reception.

Choosing the Musicians

There are many kinds of musicians playing many kinds of music. You can find perfor-mers through recommendations from friends, the caterers or the hotel, or from Yellow Pages. Ask to hear a tape, or try to hear them in action at an engagement. Make sure they are willing to perform your selections and their style suits the atmosphere you want to create. Make sure all the details are in writing – dates, times, fees, provision of equipment, and so on.

Discotheques

Many people prefer to hire a disc jockey who brings his own selection of records to the reception. As with bands, they all have their own personality and style, so try to choose someone you like and in whom you have confidence. If you want a variety of music, make sure his selection includes waltzes and foxtrots as well as modern pop music. Most disc jockeys who work regularly at weddings will have a good selection.

Hear their sound system if possible, or at least make sure that you know what system will be used and that he will provide everything which is necessary. Avoid disc jockeys who play their music too loud. People want to talk at a wedding as well as dance.

Taped Music

You can tape your own music and ask a friend to operate the equipment. Allow as much time as possible to make your musical selections and put together the tapes. You can hire or borrow the equipment. When recording, keep the volume low to avoid vibrations, and try to get a smooth flow from one piece of music to the next. You might want to make a special tape of background music to play during the meal, and another for the dancing later on. Be sure to label your tapes clearly, and include a good variety of music for all ages. Deputise someone to keep the music running smoothly and to make sure the tape does not run out just as everyone is on the dance floor. Make a note of the last piece of music on the tape case as a warning.

23 Second Marriages

SECOND MARRIAGES are generally more informal and quieter celebrations than first marriages, especially if both partners are divorced, but they are still a time to celebrate a joyous occasion with friends and family.

Many churches have strict rules about second marriages, so the ceremony is more likely to be a civil one if either of the couple is divorced. However, if you are a member of a church, talk to the minister. Some churches do allow second marriages in special circumstances, or you may be able to arrange a service of blessing after a civil ceremony.

The bride would not normally wear a white wedding dress and veil, unless it is her first wedding, although she will want something extra special. A well-cut suit or long silk dress would be suitable, usually in pastel colours, with a corsage or simple bouquet. She may not have an attendant, but if she does, there is usually only one close friend. The groom generally wears a smart suit.

If the bride's parents are hosting the occasion, they would send out the invitations, or they can be sent from the bride and groom. If the ceremony is small you may wish to invite only close family to the register office, then invite guests to a reception afterwards. You can have the invitations printed, or use pre-printed or handwritten invitations.

The type of reception you have is up to you, but again it is likely to be an informal one, with speeches and toasts kept simple and light-hearted.

If there are children from previous marriages, then obviously the couple will have spent time beforehand getting them used to the idea of the marriage and the new arrangements which will follow. Being a step-parent can be a difficult role, so try to establish a good relationship with the children as early as possible, and enlist your partner's help and support. Involve them in the ceremony, too, so that they do not feel excluded from the occasion.

Try to arrange a honeymoon if you can, away from the pressures of home. It will be a good time to confirm your new relationship together and make the wedding even more of an occasion to remember.

24 Money-Saving Ideas

Dresses

1. Wear your mother's or grandmother's dress, or borrow a wedding dress from a relative or friend.

2. Try to find a second-hand dress in an agency or through an advertisement.

3. Hire your wedding dress, and ask the chief bridesmaid to return it for you after the wedding.

4. Make your own dress or have it made by a friend or local dressmaker.

5. Some shops mark down wedding dresses at the end of the season or because the style has been discontinued. Make sure your bargain is suitable for the time of year of your wedding.

6. Order a bridesmaid's dress in white and use it as a wedding dress.

Headdress

7. Ask friends or family if they have a headdress you could borrow. Some can be adapted to suit your dress more precisely.

8. Make your own headdress. A simple wreath or cap with the veiling attached, or a white hat in any style you choose would be easiest. You can attach flowers, bows, lace and pearls to make the perfect style for you.

9. Buy a second-hand veil or headdress.

10. You and your attendants could wear flowers in your hair instead of a headdress.

Accessories

11. Buy shoes in a style that can be worn later as a dress shoe, or choose a style that can be dyed.

12. Buy your shoes at an off-season sale.

13. Borrow your shoes from another bride, but be sure they fit well and are comfortable.

14. Make your own handbag. Find a pattern for a simple drawstring bag and some pretty material to match your dress.

15. Wear underwear that you already have or borrow items you may not have such as a crinoline style petticoat.

Flowers

16. Carry a single flower, or a small nosegay and have your attendants do the same.

17. Choose flowers in season.

18. Choose popular and inexpensive flowers and keep floral arrangements to a minimum.

19. Have single flower buds in vases as centrepieces for the reception tables.

20. Transfer the ceremony flowers to the reception site, if the ceremony is not in a church.

21. If you have enough time, plant and grow your own wedding flowers and arrange them yourself.

22. Buy flowers from a nursery and arrange them yourself.

23. Decorate the ceremony or reception site with potted plants and flowers that you can later use to decorate your new home.

24. Share the cost of the flowers with other brides using the church or reception site on the same day.

25. Buy artificial or silk flowers and arrange them yourself.

Invitations

26. Buy printed invitations and fill in the relevant blanks.

27. Handwrite each guest's invitation on attractive stationery.

Food and Drink

28. Serve cocktails and hors d'oeuvres in the afternoon as an alternative to a sit-down luncheon or dinner.

29. Serve the meal buffet-style.

30. Use a sparkling wine for the toasts instead of Champagne.

31. Serve only cake and punch or Champagne at your reception.

32. Serve only Champagne, wine or punch instead of providing a variety of drinks.

33. Bake your own wedding cake.

34. Ask a friend to bake or decorate your wedding cake.

35. Borrow a cake top from a friend or use fresh flowers.

36. Borrow cake cutters, serving knives etc.

37. Cook or prepare a buffet for your guests yourself.

38. Borrow items like coffee pot, tables, chairs instead of hiring.

39. Cook part of the meal and have the rest catered.

40. Set the tables yourself.

41. Buy your food and drink from a wholesaler.

42. Ask friends or relatives to man the bar.

43. Buy ready-cooked food.

44. Buy drinks on a sale-or-return basis.

Photographs

45. Don't try to economise on black and white photographs. They are rarely used and can be more expensive than colour.

46. Ask about special effects pictures. Many photographers offer them at no additional charge.

47. Hire a professional photographer to provide a few formal photographs. Then offer to supply film and flash to a few friends to take pictures throughout the day.

48. Ask a friend to take all the wedding pictures.

49. Order the photographs to create your own wedding album, rather than buying the album itself from the photographer.

Decorations

50. Ask your family and wedding party to do the decorations, if possible on the day before the wedding.

51. If the venue is attractive, do not bother with decorations. Once the place is full of people, they will not be missed.

52. Make your own decorations, rather than buying them. A craft book at your library will give directions for making paper flowers etc.

Honeymoon

53. Travel outside the high season.

54. Go camping or caravanning.

55. Spend one or two nights in a bridal suite rather than a week somewhere.

56. If you travel by car, take a cool box for picnic food to save on lunches.

57. Ask the travel agent about special rates for honeymoon couples or discount holidays.

58. Combine camping with hotels or bed and breakfast.

Groom's Clothes

59. If you are hiring a morning suit, remember that the proper fit of the garment is more important than the price.

60. Choose a lounge suit which can be worn again.

Rings

61. Buy from a reputable wholesaler.

62. Buy from an antique shop, but be sure to get an independent professional valuation before you buy.

63. Use a family heirloom.

Music

64. Ask a friend to play the organ at the church.

65. Ask a friend to sing a solo.

66. Use taped music at the reception.

67. Ask a friend to be disc jockey.

Miscellaneous

68. Ask fewer guests to your reception or have a small reception then an evening party.

69. Reserve facilities and services early, the best of the inexpensive ones get booked quickly.

70. Save on postage by hand-delivering invitations to as many people as possible.

71. Have your reception at home.

72. Have fewer attendants.

73. Shop around and compare prices.

74. Whenever possible, buy items in sales.

75. Make sure you know exactly who is providing what at the wedding.

25 Delay or Cancellation

HOPEFULLY, there will be no hitches in your wedding plans, but it does happen. You may have to delay your wedding through illness, the loss of a job or any other reason, or you may be forced to cancel. If you do have to cancel the wedding, there is no need to give a reason to anyone but your closest family and friends.

Whatever the case, if the invitations have not been posted, you only need to notify immediate family members, your closest friends and the members of the wedding party.

If the invitations have been sent, you can notify the guests by telephone, personal note or a printed card. Do not send the information by post if the guests will not receive it at least one week before the wedding date so they have plenty of time to change arrangements, and in case the post is delayed. The wording on a card should be something like:

Mr and Mrs Robert Jones announce
that the marriage of their daughter
Susan Mary
to
Mr Daniel George Smith
will be postponed until. . . .
/will not take place.

As well as informing your guests, you must contact all the suppliers you have already booked, even if you have not yet paid a deposit. If your wedding is being postponed, ask if their service is available on the new date. If it is not, you should ask for any deposit to be refunded and start looking for a new supplier.

If the ceremony is cancelled, return any gifts you have received, including your engagement ring. If the bridesmaids are paying for their own dresses and lose their deposit, you should reimburse them.

Minor Accidents

Everyone dreads things going wrong on their big day, and obviously you will be doing your utmost to avoid problems. But if you do rip your dress or damage a bit of the cake icing, try to keep a sense of proportion. You will be disappointed, but it does not make any difference to the real purpose of the day, and probably no-one else will even notice!

26 Wedding Customs

JOINING couples in marriage is a tradition which dates back thousands of years, and is a custom which is steeped in ritualistic significance. Nowadays, we do not pay much attention to superstitions, and often do not know why things are done in a particular way. But the origins of many of the customs which survive today are far in the past, and were originally introduced not merely for enjoyment or convenience, but with a specific purpose, usually associated with warding off evil and bringing good luck, prosperity and children to the newly-married couple. Here are some old traditions you might find interesting and amusing.

Marriage

Originally, 'marriage' was often more like kidnap. A man would seize his chosen woman from her family and carry her off to keep house and bear children for him. It did not make a lot of difference whether she was willing or not!

A wife, of course, was a valuable asset as she could cook, clean and bring up a family. Fathers began to realise that their unmarried daughters were a saleable asset, and became more protective. Prospective husbands had to show that they could look after the girl and they began to offer valuable presents to the family, or to work off the price of the daughter's hand in marriage. The most famous example of this, of course, is Jacob in the Bible who worked for seven years in order to marry Rachel. Rather than marry off his youngest daughter first, her father substituted her sister Leah, and Jacob had to work a further seven years in order to marry his chosen wife.

Later, fathers began to offer a dowry to their daughter's husband. This was an insurance against divorce, as the woman now brought something of her own into the marriage, and the husband could only control the dowry as long as they stayed married.

In some societies, children were engaged to one another when they were very young. Contracts were drawn up detailing all the arrangements, and these were considered legally binding. If one family backed out of the arrangements, they could forfeit half their property.

Dresses and Veils

Prior to the 19th century, a bride would be married in her best dress, sometimes one which had been handed down through the generations, or sometimes her national costume. There was therefore no special colour for a wedding dress until the choice of a white dress became popular after Anne of Brittany married Louis XII in white. The colour became popular as a symbol of purity and was thought to ward off evil.

As for other colours, this old anonymous poem gives some ideas.

Marry in white, you've chosen aright.

Marry in blue, your love is true.

Marry in pearl, you'll live in a whirl.

Marry in brown, you'll live out of town.

Marry in red, you'd be better off dead.

Marry in yellow, ashamed of the fellow.

Marry in green, ashamed to be seen.

Marry in pink, your spirits will sink.

Since time immemorial, veils have been thought to protect the wearer from evil. Since brides were thought to be particularly vulnerable to evil spirits on their wedding day, it became customary for them to wear veils. In some Eastern wedding ceremonies both bride and groom are protected by placing a veil or curtain between them.

In the case of arranged marriages, especially those between children, the bride and groom had often never seen one another before the wedding day. The bride would wear a veil right through the ceremony until the couple were declared husband and wife, only then lifting it to reveal her face to the bridegroom. Today, if the bride wears a veil over her face, it is lifted immediately after she and her groom are declared husband and wife.

The Wedding Party

The custom of the bride and groom surrounding themselves with a wedding party of close friends originates in the days when the bride was captured from her family. The groom took a group of supporters with him to distract the bride's family while he whisked her away. Once the bride had been successfully captured, he sent his 'best man' to soothe her family's tempers! At the same time, the bride needed close friends around her to provide comfort and support in her new situation.

Later, when brides were no longer captured, the wedding party became seen as a way of warding off evil spirits. The women all dressed in the same way as the bride, and the men in the same way as the groom in order to confuse the evil spirits as to the identity of the bridal couple. In early Roman times the wedding party had a further role in protecting the bridal couple's money during the wedding celebrations.

Customs and Traditions

There are many wedding customs and traditions, and it is interesting to know the origins of some of those that are most commonly followed.

Many brides insist on wearing 'something blue', but fewer will know that the custom comes from ancient Israel, where a bride wore a blue ribbon as a symbol of her fidelity.

The sharing of wine and food has long been significant in many cultures. In ancient times a couple were considered to be married when they ate and drank together, and the sharing of wine and communion is part of many Christian ceremonies today. The ritual drinking of wine also features as a part of Jewish wedding ceremonies.

A canopy appears in both Jewish and Chinese weddings, as a symbol of the home the bridal couple are setting up together, and as a way of showing respect to them. In the case of Jewish weddings the couple stand under a chuppah, while the Chinese use an umbrella.

Superstitions

The day of the week you marry has superstitions surrounding it, although for most people, it is a question of convenience!

Monday for health,

Tuesday for wealth,

Wednesday, the best day of all.

Thursday for losses,

Friday for crosses,

Saturday, no luck at all!

The month is also supposed to be significant. June became popular because ancient Greeks and Romans honoured Juno, the goddess of love and marriage. May, on the other hand, was unlucky because it was the month in which the Romans celebrated the feast of the dead, and the festival of the goddess of chastity.

These are all supposed to be signs of good luck:

- the bride placing a coin in her shoe for wealth;
- the bride being awakened by the song of a bird;
- sunny weather.

These are all signs of bad luck:

- to wear the wedding ring before the ceremony;
- to wear an opal, unless you were born in October;
- to wear green, unless you are Irish;
- to buy the engagement and wedding rings at the same time;
- for the groom to see the bride in her wedding dress before they are married.

Food and Cake

The bride and groom sharing a meal after the wedding ceremony has always been seen as a confirmation of their new status. In fact, in early Rome, the marriage contract was not legally binding until a couple had shared bread together.

Tossing and Throwing

Tossing confetti at the bride and groom is a relatively new idea, and since it can make such a mess of a churchyard and is often not allowed there, we may well go back to the older ideas of tossing rice or grain, both of which are symbols of food and of children. Although you can now buy confetti which birds will eat, so always choose that in preference to the 'litter' variety.

If you are used to throwing confetti and decide to throw rice, remember that it is a great deal heavier and should be thrown into the air and allowed to fall gently.

Rings

The ring has always been a symbol of continuity and unity, and very early in history was adopted as a suitable symbol for a married couple.

Grooms used to present their future brides with an object of value when they were betrothed, and this was often a family ring. At the wedding itself he also gave her a gift, and this has developed into the custom of giving a ring.

Most couples wear their wedding rings on their left hand, probably because most people are right-handed, so the ring is less inconvenient. More romantically a vein is supposed to run from the third finger of the left hand directly to the heart, so this became the most popular finger on which to wear the wedding ring.

Celebrations

Feasts are a natural way of celebrating and allowing the families of the bridal couple to join in the festivities and get to know one another. They traditionally also involved ritual dances, some of which were designed to ward off evil, others to bless the ceremony. Often the bride and groom take the first dance. This probably originates in a puritanical European tradition; the couple had the first three dances together and were closely observed to see whether there was any premature love-making!

Flowers

Carrying flowers is obviously decorative, but it may also hark back to the belief that a bouquet of strong smelling herbs from the onion family, such as garlic or chives, would drive away evil spirits.

Today many flowers symbolise something. Here are a few:

apple blossoms – better things to come;

ivy – good luck and eternal fidelity;

lily – purity;

rose – beauty and happiness;

orange blossom – fertility and happiness.

The Honeymoon

In the days when a bridegroom captured his bride, the couple hid from her parents until the search was dropped. They would hide for one cycle of the moon while drinking honeyed wine. Not many couples could afford this luxury today, but a honeymoon is still something rather special.

Carrying her over the threshold may also originate from this time, as a way of stopping her from running away.

27 The Honeymoon

A HONEYMOON is your chance to get away from it all, relax and enjoy each other's company. Even if you only have the time and money for a weekend break, treat yourself to that. It will give you a chance to wind down after the excitement of the wedding, and set you up for your new life together.

Time and Money

Before you decide what kind of holiday to look for, you should work out how much you can afford to spend and how much time you can take for your honeymoon. If you have combined your wedding plans with your summer holiday, you may have two weeks or more and a reasonable budget, but if you plan another holiday in the same year, you may prefer to choose a shorter or simpler honeymoon.

When thinking about the cost, bear in mind not only the major costs such as transport, accommodation and meals, but also other expenses such as drinks, entertainment, souvenirs, insurance and so on.

What Kind of Honeymoon?

Naturally you must both enjoy the honeymoon, so it is important to find time to talk about what you would like to do. Looking at the questions below should help you to plan the perfect trip.

What is your honeymoon budget? _____

How much time do you have? _____

Do you want to travel abroad? _____

Will you travel by train, car, bicycle or aeroplane? _____

Do you want to stay in one place or tour? _____

What style of holiday do you prefer:

    luxurious? _____

    adventurous? _____

    meeting new people? _____

    lazy? _____

    active? _____

What type of atmosphere do you want:

    big city? _____

    countryside? _____

    foreign culture? _____

places of historical significance? _____

sunshine and beaches? _____

ski resort? _____

night life? _____

Where do you prefer to stay:

a luxury hotel? _____

a moderately priced hotel? _____

a flat or villa? _____

a tent or caravan? _____

don't care? _____

If you don't already have a special place in mind, ask friends and family for suggestions. Look in the library travel section. Go to the travel agents to look through the brochures and ask advice. Always choose a reputable travel agent who is a member of ABTA and covered by their insurance bond should anything go wrong.

Making the Plans

Make your arrangements and reservations early, especially if you are travelling in high season and choosing a popular holiday resort. If you are booking late, be guided by a good travel agent – they may be able to steer you to a bargain holiday. Find out about any necessary innoculations or special regulations so that you can arrange them as early as possible to avoid reactions too near your wedding day.

Remember that you will be tired after an exciting and exhausting day, so it may be a good idea to stay in a nearby hotel for the first night, then fly off on your honeymoon the following day.

Keep all your travel documents together safely and arrange passport details if necessary. Have them ready when you leave the reception – the best man can take care of them for you.

Pack well in advance if you can, to avoid having to worry about packing at the last minute when you have other things on your mind. Try to avoid overpacking. Find out what weather and conditions to expect and pack suitable things with plenty of mix-and-match clothes in non-crease fabrics. Arrange for the best man to put your cases in the car ready for your departure from the reception. Allow plenty of time to reach the hotel, station or airport, and remember that you may have to stop to tidy up your car if it has been decorated. If you dread this idea, hide it well or arrange to leave the reception by taxi.

Before you Leave

Make sure that someone, probably your mother, will take care of the gifts, particularly cheques, if you are leaving straight away. The best man should be responsible for returning any hired suits etc., or your mother or the chief bridesmaid if you have hired your wedding dress.

Try to arrange for someone to check on your house or flat while you are away. Make sure there are no milk or papers being delivered, and ask a friend or neighbour to collect your post. If you have any security lighting etc. set it up before you go, and remember all the normal security precautions you would expect to take before going away on any holiday.

28 Financial Responsibilities

AS A MARRIED couple, you may decide to change your financial arrangements, and this chapter will give you some guidelines. Remember that the competition between banks and building societies means that new types of accounts are becoming available all the time, so shop around and get up-to-the-minute advice before making your decisions.

Joint Finances

You will want to make financial arrangements suitable to both of you and your incomes. You probably know already whether you both wish to continue working, so will know your joint income. Think about what your outgoings will be: rent or mortgage, rates, power bills, telephone, entertaining, food and so on. Will you both run cars? Will you be able to afford holidays? You can then work out a financial plan, and set goals for the future.

Choose your bank account arrangements to suit both of you and make the necessary arrangements. You may prefer to keep separate accounts, or change to a joint account. It may be easier to have separate accounts, for example, if one of you will travel a great deal, or you may feel it is important to have your own personal funds. On the other hand, some couples feel it is easier to think of the money as belonging to you mutually if you have one account. If you have two cheque books for one account, be careful to keep track of the balance.

If you have one account, then there are no arguments over who pays the bills. If you choose separate accounts, you can decide that the mortgage, rates and heating bills are paid from one account, for example, and the telephone, electricity and food bills are paid from the other.

You may also wish to have a savings account. There are many kinds offered by both banks and building societies and you can choose to pay in a regular amount each month, or simply pay in whenever you have some money over.

Credit

Credit agreements can still be held in either of your names individually after you are married, or in joint names. It is important to remember that if a loan is in joint names you are each personally responsible for its repayment if the other fails to pay up. In the case of a mortgage, which will be the largest loan for any couple, it is nevertheless wiser to have it in joint names to help avoid any dispute over ownership of the home should a divorce ever take place.

Most lenders will require some evidence of your ability to repay their loan. This may be a statement of your income, or you may be asked to provide some collateral. In particular, any lender granting a mortgage will take a charge on your house. This means that they would be able to sell your home should you fail to keep up the repayments.

If you do fall behind with any payments – whether mortgage, rent, hire purchase or other credit – talk to the people involved. Explain your situation and ask to extend the term of the loan and make smaller payments, or some similar arrangements.

Income Tax

For most couples, income tax is deducted at source as PAYE. You must inform your tax office of your marriage, since tax is calculated on your joint income. However, from April 1990 husbands and wives will receive separate tax returns to fill in, and be responsible for paying their own tax. Ask your local tax office for details.

Pensions and Insurance

Pension and insurance schemes are designed so that by making relatively small regular contributions you can claim on the fund at some future date when specified eventualities put you in financial difficulties.

It is important to provide for your retirement. You can join your employer's pension plan or you can pay into the government scheme or choose a private plan. Find out whether your marriage makes any difference to your payments or returns.

Life insurance is a safeguard for your dependants, and is especially important if you have a family. You should have enough cover to replace your salary for as long as possible, take care of children, and pay as many of the bills as possible. Both of you should be covered, since if you are both working your income will be much reduced if either of you should die, while if one of you is caring for the children, whichever of you is widowed would either have to give up work or pay someone else to keep house. Ask for advice from a reputable firm about the type of policy which would suit you best.

House buildings insurance is obligatory if you buy a house, but you should always insure the contents of your home against possible loss, such as from theft, fire etc. Make sure it covers the value of your property at their replacement value as new, and upgrade the coverage every year to keep up with inflation. All policies differ, so watch out for exceptions or penalty clauses, such as paying the first £50 of any claim yourself. Again, shop around and take advice from a reputable source as to the best policy to suit your needs. It is easy to underestimate the value of your possessions, so take a notebook and go round the house room by room noting everything you have. Then look at a mail order or store catalogue and mark in approximate prices. You will probably be astonished at how much is tied up in the simplest household items, such as sheets, towels, kitchen equipment, let alone carpets and furniture. In most policies, you have to list any items over a certain value, or items which are to be insured whether they are in or out of the house, such as jewellery. Take pictures of particularly valuable items, or use security markers as an extra safeguard.

Making a Will

It is a good idea to make a will to make sure your property is divided as you wish it to be after your death. Unless your affairs are complicated, a solicitor can draw up a will for a relatively low fee. Once you have a property and a family, your estate may be more complicated and valuable than you think. Bear in mind when making specific bequests that they should be written in a way to protect your spouse and children should the value of your estate drop.

Ask for a recommendation when choosing a solicitor, or go to a reputable local firm. Get an estimate in advance of the expected costs. Don't take up more of your solicitor's time than necessary, because that time will cost you money.

Buying or Renting a Property

If you are going to rent a property after you are married, you will have to sign an agreement detailing your obligations, when the rent is due, who is responsible for repairs etc. It should also state what notice must be given to terminate the tenancy, how long you can remain there and so on. Find out from the previous tenant if possible whether the landlord is approachable, whether he deals with problems swiftly and efficiently, or if there have been any difficulties.

If you are able to buy a house, take good advice on the amount of money you can afford to borrow as a mortgage. Shop around the banks and building societies to see who offers the best options, but beware of borrowing too much and then being unable to make repayments. Remember that you will be responsible for all bills relating to the house: repairs and maintenance, decorating, plumbing and so on. It might be a good time to invest in a D-I-Y handbook!

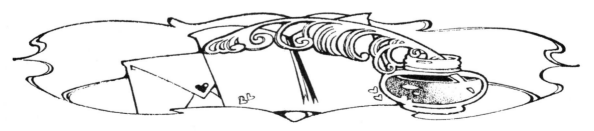

29 Changing your Name

AFTER THE wedding, most brides decide to take their husband's surname as their own, although it is not a legal requirement. You may keep your own name, use your husband's name, use both (using your maiden name for professional use, for example) or hyphenate the two names.

If you hyphenate the names, you should both use the same name. If you are using both names, remember that you may require identification for both which could be confusing – it depends on the circumstances. It is often a good idea for you both to use one name in financial dealings since it can make things simpler.

There are all sorts of people you should notify if you do change your name. Consult the checklist at the back of the book as a starting point and add any others you may think of. You can write and photocopy a standard letter for many people to make it easier. Some may require copies of the wedding certificate, or you may need to supply new signatures.

If you are going abroad on your honeymoon and your passport is in your maiden name, you should take your marriage certificate with you. If you want a new passport in your married name, you will have to apply to the Passport Office, Clive House, Petty France, London SW1. You will not receive the passport until you are legally married, but it may be sent to the appropriate minister or registrar to give to you after the wedding.

30 After the Wedding

EVERY BRIDE spares some thought to what married life will be like. How will you get on when you are living together? Will you change? Will your relationship be less special? Considering how important a step you are about to take, it is not surprising that everyone has questions.

Of course, no one knows what your married life will be like. But one thing is certain: change. Married or not, as we grow older, we mature and are mellowed (or otherwise!) by our experiences. We meet and make new friends, lose touch with others, and strengthen the ties with those closest to us.

As you mature and share experiences, your characters will develop, and so will your relationship and the way you see each other. This is nothing to be wary of, but something to welcome. Life would become very boring if things were the same all the time.

You may look at other married couples now and wonder why they no longer seem 'head over heels' in love as you are. But because their relationship is different and they have grown comfortable with each other, does not mean that their love is any less. It is just different.

Starting life together is a new experience, and will involve a period of getting to know each other. You will have to get used to living together, sharing experiences, and learning about each other. It may even involve a few eye-openers if you discover things about your partner that you had never noticed before. Odd little habits which noticed now and again were endearing, may become annoying when they confront you every day. Don't be put off. This happens to everyone, and is all part of your readjustment to life as a married person. Try to keep things in perspective, and remember that you have odd habits too!

Try not to be in too much of a hurry. Take your time to get used to each other, and take a relaxed attitude to your new life. Keep things in perspective, keep an open mind, and try to remember that you both have a point of view to consider. In this way you can get through any problems, see the other's point of view and see the importance of small things to the value of your complete relationship.

Never expect your partner to change instantly, just because you are married. Neither of you will be magically transformed into the perfect couple just because you are wearing each other's rings. Be patient with yourself and your partner, and try to fit in with each other, rather than expecting sudden alterations.

Your marriage will be what you make it. It is easy to take one another for granted and get wrapped up in everyday living. But keep an eye on how you are treating each other. If you notice a small problem and take action to do something about it, you can get back on an even keel quickly and easily, and avoid potential problems.

It can be a mistake to think that because you are married you should do everything together. You are still two individuals with your own interests, so keep up your evening classes, sports or social activities with other friends. You can then both bring more into the relationship.

The role of your families may also change when you marry. They can be very supportive and helpful, especially when you are starting out. Or they can be a bit of a nuisance. Talk about how you feel about your families, and it will put the lie to those dreadful mother-in-law jokes!

Communication is the key to keeping a developing relationship fresh. Learn to talk about things that concern you, and you will be able to smooth out the bad times and enjoy the good times to the full.

31 Wedding Anniversaries

MOST PEOPLE like to remember what a wonderful wedding day they had by celebrating their wedding anniversaries with presents, cards and perhaps an evening out. It is a good time to think about your lives together and prepare for the coming year.

Traditionally, certain materials are associated with particular years of marriage; the idea being that those particular items from your wedding gifts would have worn out that year and so will need replacing! You therefore choose a gift made out of the relevant material. Some years this is easier than others!

First	Cotton
Second	Paper
Third	Leather
Fourth	Books or silk
Fifth	Wood
Sixth	Sugar
Seventh	Wool or copper
Eighth	Bronze
Ninth	Pottery
Tenth	Tin
Eleventh	Steel
Twelfth	Silk and fine linen
Thirteenth	Lace
Fourteenth	Ivory
Fifteenth	Crystal
Twentieth	China
Twenty-fifth	Silver
Thirtieth	Pearl
Thirty-fifth	Coral
Fortieth	Ruby
Forty-fifth	Sapphire
Fiftieth	Gold
Fifty-fifth	Emerald
Sixtieth or Seventy-fifth	Diamond

32 My Wedding Plans

THIS SECTION of the book is designed as your personal wedding checklist to help you to organise everything and to make sure that nothing is forgotten for your perfect day.

Every wedding is different, so check the lists carefully as you make your plans and amend them to suit your individual needs. If you keep all the information together in one place you are less likely to lose that vital telephone number, and if you fill in details and tick off when things are done, you have a better chance of remembering everything. But do keep the book in a safe place; don't leave it lying around!

So enjoy your wedding plans, and have a wonderful day. Savour every moment and it will be a day full of memories which you will treasure.

The wedding of _____

to _____ _____

on _____

at _____

at _____ o'clock

and afterwards at _____

Notes and Ideas

Use these pages as your rough notepad while you are thinking about the sort of wedding you would like. You can stick in pictures from magazines, jot down notes or drawings, ideas and costs, queries to follow up or questions to ask. Use pencil, then you can rub out as you change your mind and still have room for all the new ideas.

You will soon begin to see your personal wedding plan falling into shape, and will be able to embark on the real plan in all its detail.

Wedding style (formal or informal): _____

Budget: _____

Wedding party
Best man:
Chief bridesmaid:
Bridesmaids:
Page boys:

Ceremony
Venue:
Date/time:

Reception
Style:
Venue:
Food and drink:
Music:

Invitations and stationery:

Wedding dress:

Bridesmaids' dresses:

Men's clothes:

Flowers:

Photographs:

Rings:

Cake:

Cars:

Honeymoon:

Planning Timetable

It is impossible to be too specific about when you should do each part of your planning, since it will depend on the style of wedding and how you like to organise things. But take a tip from most brides who say that it is best to start organising as early as possible to give yourself time to shop around and time to plan everything exactly as you want it.

This outline below is based on having six months to plan the event, and gives suggestions on how to organise the time. When you have decided on the details of your wedding, adapt the outline to suit your individual needs, and use it to make sure nothing is forgotten.

Six Months Before

- [ ] Make a preliminary, then an actual budget
- [ ] Decide on the kind of wedding you want
- [ ] Set the date
- [ ] Choose and book the location of the ceremony
- [ ] Meet the minister to discuss and finalise details
- [ ] Arrange for the banns to be published or note when to apply for the licence
- [ ] Arrange for the banns to be published in the groom's parish
- [ ] Choose and book the reception venue
- [ ] Draw up the guest list
- [ ] Choose the bridesmaids, best man and ushers
- [ ] Choose and book the caterer
- [ ] Choose and book the bar/drinks supplier
- [ ] Choose and book the photographer
- [ ] Choose and book the florist
- [ ] Choose and book the car
- [ ] Choose and book the musicians/disco

Four Months Before

☐	Choose and buy your dress and headdress
☐	Choose and buy your shoes, underwear, accessories
☐	Choose and buy the bridesmaids' dresses
☐	Arrange for the formal wear for the groom and principal men
☐	Plan and book the honeymoon
☐	Prepare a wedding list or register with a department store
☐	Order invitations, order of service sheets, cake boxes, seating cards and other stationery
☐	Make sure your mother and the groom's mother have selected their outfits
☐	Make sure you have somewhere to live after the wedding and start shopping for furnishings etc.
☐	Order the cake
☐	

Two Months Before

☐	Choose your gifts to the groom and your attendants
☐	Make sure the groom has chosen a gift for the best man and ushers
☐	Address and send the invitations
☐	Buy the wedding rings
☐	Buy your going-away outfit and any new outfits for the honeymoon
☐	Practise your make-up
☐	

☐ Make an appointment with the hairdresser for the day before the wedding, and decide how you will wear your hair

☐ Discuss and finalise the photography arrangements

☐ Discuss and finalise the floral arrangements and bouquets

☐

☐

☐

☐

One Month Before

☐ Make sure the groom has his hair cut

☐ Have a final dress fitting for yourself and your attendants

☐ Collect licence

☐ Finalise rehearsal arrangements

☐ Arrange pre-wedding parties

☐ Make arrangements for transport and hospitality for any attendants travelling some distance to the wedding

☐ Make all transport arrangements for the wedding day

☐ Confirm all appointments and arrangements

☐ Buy ribbons for the wedding cars

☐

☐

Two Weeks Before

- ☐ Record gifts and write thank-yous as they come in
- ☐ Prepare newspaper announcements
- ☐ Make seating plan for the reception and place cards for the tables
- ☐ Arrange for your name changes on driving licence, at work, insurance policies, bank account etc.
- ☐ Begin moving into your new home

One Week Before

- ☐ Rehearsal
- ☐ Make sure all attendants know their duties and when and where they are supposed to be at each venue
- ☐ Make sure the groom and best man know whom to thank in their speeches
- ☐ Arrange for a display of gifts
- ☐ Wrap gifts for the groom and attendants
- ☐ Give final numbers and seating arrangements to the caterer
- ☐ Practise make-up and hair with dress and headdress
- ☐ Manicure or beauty treatment
- ☐ Make sure the groom has all his clothes ready
- ☐ Confirm arrangements for the car
- ☐ Confirm arrangements for the flowers

☐	Confirm arrangements for the reception venue
☐	Confirm arrangements for the photographs
☐	Confirm arrangements for musicians/disco
☐	Collect banns certificate from groom's minister
☐	Cake delivered
☐	Pack for the honeymoon
☐	Pack honeymoon documents
☐	Make sure the going-away car is serviced and will be full of petrol
☐	Allocate as many jobs to others as possible for the wedding day
☐	Enjoy the pre-wedding parties
☐	Make arrangements for the return of any hired items
☐	Make arrangements for the announcement and photograph to be sent to the paper
☐	Make sure best man has/knows when to collect buttonholes, order of service sheets, transport arrangements etc
☐	
☐	

After the Wedding

☐	Complete outstanding thank-you letters
☐	Order photographs
☐	Write to thank your parents and the groom's parents for arranging the wedding
☐	
☐	

Budget Sheets

	Estimate	Final Cost	Deposit Paid	Balance Paid
Church/Register Office				
Fees				
Choir				
Organist				
Soloist				
Licence				
Bells				
Other				
TOTALS				
Reception				
Rent				
Decorations				
Furniture				
Music				
Other				
TOTALS				
Food and Drink				
Caterer				
Cake				
Crockery				
Cutlery				
Service				
Drinks				
Glasses				

	Estimate	Final Cost	Deposit Paid	Balance Paid
Barman				
Other				
TOTALS				
Invitations and Stationery				
Invitations and envelopes				
Postage				
Place cards				
Order of service sheets				
Cake boxes				
Other				
TOTALS				
Clothes				
Wedding dress				
Headdress				
Shoes and accessories				
Bridesmaids' dresses/accesories				
Groom's clothes/accesories				
Going-away outfits				
Other				
TOTALS				
Flowers				
Bride's bouquet				
Bridesmaids' bouquets				
Buttonholes				
Coursages				
Church				

	Estimate	Final Cost	Deposit Paid	Balance Paid
Reception				
Other				
TOTALS				
Photographer				
Wedding package				
Album				
Additional prints				
Additional albums				
Video				
Other				
TOTALS				
Honeymoon				
Travel				
Accommodation				
Clothes				
Spending money				
Documentation				
Other				
TOTALS				
Miscellaneous				
Rings				
Cars				
Hairdresser				
Make-up				
Presents				
Other				
TOTALS				

Draft Guest List

List the names of those you would like to invite so that you can get some idea of numbers before finalising your guest list. Start the list with your parents, then consult the groom and his parents.

Total number agreed _____

Definite	Probable	Possible

Definite	Probable	Possible

Guest List and Present Record

Total number invited: adults _____

children _____

Total number accepted: adults _____

children _____

Special needs: _____

_____

Name	Address and Telephone	Invite Sent	Reply Received (√ or x)	Details of Present Received	Thank you Sent

Name	Address and Telephone	Invite Sent	Reply Received (√ or x)	Details of Present Received	Thank you Sent

Name	Address and Telephone	Invite Sent	Reply Received (√ or x)	Details of Present Received	Thank you Sent

Name	Address and Telephone	Invite Sent	Reply Received (√ or x)	Details of Present Received	Thank you Sent

Presents from Friends not Attending the Wedding

Name	Address	Present Received	Thank you Sent

Name	Address	Present Received	Thank you Sent

Invitations and Stationery

Supplier _____

Address _____

_____

Telephone _____

Invitation wording _____

_____

_____

_____

Style _____

Paper colour _____

Ink colour _____

Illustrations _____

Number ordered _____

Order of Service sheets _____

(Provided typed copy separately for the printer)

Number ordered _____

Thank you cards _____

Cake boxes _____

Place cards _____

Other _____

_____

_____

Date for proofs to be checked _____

Date for collection _____

Church or Register Office

Church _____

Minister _____

Address _____

_____

Telephone _____

Date booked _____

Time of ceremony _____

Banns to be read _____

Processional music _____

Music while signing the register _____

Recessional music _____

Address _____

Prayers _____

Readings _____

Organ _____

Choir _____

Soloist _____

Hymns _____

Bells _____

Rehearsal date _____

Photographs allowed _____

_____

Confetti allowed _____

Flowers _____

Other brides _____

_____

Licence obtained _____

Groom's church _____

Minister _____

Address _____

_____

Telephone _____

Banns to be read _____

Reception

Venue _____

Address _____

_____

Telephone _____

Date booked _____

Time _____

Size of room _____

Decorations _____

Parking _____

Heating_____

Toilets/cloakroom facilities _____

Changing facilities for bride _____

Insurance _____

Cleaning up _____

Tables provided and set up _____

Chairs provided and arranged _____

Kitchen facilities _____

Cutlery and crockery _____

Glasses _____

Table linen _____

Bar facilities/drinks _____

Facilities for musicians/etc. _____

_____

Musicians/discotheque _____

Address _____

_____

Telephone _____

Times booked _____

First dance _____

Special requests _____

Food and Drink

Caterer _____

Address _____

_____

Telephone _____

Menu selected _____

_____

_____

Number of guests: adults _____

children _____

Special needs: _____

Number of waitresses _____

Are waitresses in uniform? _____

What will happen to leftovers? _____

Tea/coffee _____

Will they cut and serve the cake? _____

Caterer to supply   **Quantity/Details**

	Caterer to supply	Quantity/Details
☐	Crockery	_____
☐	Cutlery	_____
☐	Napkins	_____
☐	Table linen	_____
☐	Cake knife	_____
☐	Waitresses	_____
☐	Table decorations	_____
☐	Clearing up	_____
☐	Aperitifs	_____
☐	Wine	_____
☐	Champagne	_____

Caterer to supply   **Quantity/Details**

| | Glasses
| | _____

_____

_____

Reception venue _____

Caterer's arrival time _____

Bar facilities _____

Barman _____

Address _____

_____

Telephone _____

Drinks before the meal _____

_____

Drinks with the meal _____

_____

Toasts _____

Drinks after the meal _____

_____

Soft drinks _____

_____

Wedding Cake

Supplier _____

Address _____

_____

Telephone _____

Style of cake _____

_____

Shape/size _____

Number of tiers _____

Decoration for top _____

_____

Delivery date and time _____

Delivery address _____

_____

Wedding Rings

Supplier _____

Address _____

_____

Telephone _____

Date rings ordered _____

Details to be engraved _____

_____

Date for collection _____

Wedding Dress and Bridesmaids' Dresses

Bride's dress supplier _____

Address _____

_____

Telephone _____

Dates for fittings _____

Alterations _____

Date for collection _____

Date for return if hired _____

To be returned by _____

☐ Dress colour _____

Style _____

Fabric _____

Embroidery/trimmings _____

Bodice/neckline _____

Waist/sash _____

Sleeves _____

Skirt _____

Length/hemline _____

☐ Headdress colour _____

Style _____

Fabric _____

Embroidery/trimmings _____

Veil _____

☐ Shoes

☐ Underwear and stockings

☐ Accessories

☐ Jewellery

☐ Make-up and nail varnish

☐ Old, new, borrowed, blue

Bridesmaids' dresses supplier _____

Address _____

_____

Telephone _____

☐ Dresses _____

Colour _____

Style _____

Fabric _____

Embroidery/trimmings _____

Bodice/neckline _____

Waist/sash _____

Sleeves _____

Skirt _____

Length/hemline _____

☐ Headdresses

☐ Shoes

☐ Underwear and stockings

☐ Accessories

☐ Jewellery

Going-away outfit _____

Flowers

Florist _____

Address _____

_____

Telephone _____

Style of flowers _____

_____

_____

Special notes _____

Colour scheme _____

_____

_____

Bride's Bouquet

Colour _____

Style _____

Bridesmaids' Bouquets

Colour _____

Style _____

Number _____

Corsages

Colour _____

Style _____

Number _____

Buttonholes

Colour _____

Style _____

Number _____

Delivery date and time _____

Delivery address _____

_____

Church/Register Office Flowers

Colour _____

Style _____

Number of arrangements _____

Delivery date and time _____

Delivery address _____

_____

Reception Flowers

Colour _____

Style _____

Number of arrangements _____

Delivery date and time _____

Delivery address _____

_____

Groom's Clothes

Formalwear supplier _____

Address _____

_____

Telephone _____

Dates for fittings _____

Alterations _____

Date for collection _____

Date for return _____

To be returned by _____

Colours _____

Style _____

☐ Suit

☐ Waistcoat

☐ Shirt

☐ Tie

☐ Shoes

☐ Gloves

☐ Top hat

☐ Socks and underwear

☐ Cufflinks and jewellery

Going-away outfit _____

Cars

Supplier _____

Address _____

_____

Telephone _____

Car _____

Back-up car _____

Chauffeur _____

To collect bride and bride's father

From _____

At _____

_____

Ceremony venue _____

_____

Reception venue _____

_____

Number to telephone in emergency _____

Special notes _____

_____

Taxi firms telephone for emergency 1. _____

2. _____

3. _____

Car for bridesmaids _____

_____

Photographs

Photographer _____

Address _____

_____

Telephone _____

Proofs ready by _____

Before the Ceremony

Arrival time _____   Location _____

Bride

☐	Close up
☐	With mother
☐	With father
☐	With mother and father
☐	With family
☐	With bridesmaids
☐	At dressing table

☐	At gift table
☐	Full length
☐	Adjusting veil
☐	With flowers
☐	Leaving with father
☐	
☐	

At the Church/Register Office

Arrival time _____   Location _____

☐	Groom
☐	Groom with best man
☐	Groom with ushers
☐	Bridesmaids
☐	Pages

☐	Guests arriving
☐	Bride arriving with father
☐	Bride outside church
☐	
☐	

During the Ceremony

☐ Signing the register   ☐ At the church door

☐ Leaving the church

Outside the Church/Register Office

Bride

☐ Alone

☐ With bridesmaids

☐ With bride's parents

Bride and Groom

☐ Together outside church   ☐ With groom's family

☐ With bride's parents   ☐ With friends

☐ With groom's parents   ☐ Guests throwing rice etc.

☐ With both sets of parents   ☐ Leaving for reception

☐ With parents, best man and   ☐ In car

bridesmaids   ☐

☐ With best man and bridesmaids   ☐

☐ With bride's family   ☐

At the Reception

Arrival time _____   Location _____

Bride and Groom

☐ Arriving   ☐ With groom's parents

☐ In receiving line   ☐ With both sets of parents

☐ With bride's parents   ☐ With special friends

☐ With godparents

☐ Cutting cake

☐ During toasts

☐ During first dance

Leaving for the Honeymoon

☐ Leaving the reception

☐ Throwing bouquet

☐ Getting into car

☐ Car leaving

Miscellaneous/Special Effects

Video photographer _____

Address _____

_____

Telephone _____

Before the ceremony _____

During the ceremony _____

Outside the church _____

_____

At the reception _____

Special notes _____

Photograph Order for Guests

Name	Address	Telephone	Proof Number	Size	Quantity

Wedding List

Use this sample wedding list to give you ideas. You can cross out items, or add others as you wish. Take a copy of the pages to send to people who ask to see the list. They will tick the list and you can up-date the book when it is returned. That way, you will always have an accurate copy and will help to avoid duplication.

		Style/Colour/Make			Style/Colour/Make
Bathroom					
☐	Bath mat set		☐		
☐	Bathroom cabinet		☐		
☐	Bath sheets		☐		
☐	Bath towels		☐		
☐	Hand towels		☐		
☐	Scales		☐		
☐			☐		
Bedrooms					
☐	Bed		☐		
☐	Bed linen		☐		
☐	Bedspread		☐		
☐	Blankets		☐		
☐	Duvet		☐		
☐	Electric blanket		☐		
☐	Mirror		☐		
☐	Pillows		☐		
☐	Radio alarm		☐		
☐	Teasmade		☐		

Style/Colour/Make   **Style/Colour/Make**

Living room

- [ ] Bookcase
- [ ] Coffee table
- [ ] Cushions
- [ ] Magazine rack
- [ ] Standard lamp
- [ ] Suite
- [ ] Table lamp
- [ ] Television
- [ ] Video
- [ ]

Dining room

- [ ] Cutlery
- [ ] Dinner service
- [ ] Glassware
- [ ] Place mats
- [ ] Table linen
- [ ] Table mats
- [ ] Tea service
- [ ] Wine cooler
- [ ] Wine rack
- [ ]

Style/Colour/Make   **Style/Colour/Make**

Kitchen

☐ Apron	☐ Microwave cooker
☐ Baking tins	☐ Microwave cookware
☐ Bread bin	☐ Mixing bowls
☐ Bread board and knife	☐ Oven
☐ Buckets/bowls etc.	☐ Rolling pin
☐ Can opener	☐ Saucepans
☐ Carving knife	☐ Scales
☐ Casserole dishes	☐ Slow cooker
☐ Cheese board	☐ Soufflé dishes
☐ Coffee grinder	☐ Spice rack
☐ Coffee percolator/maker	☐ Storage jars
☐ Cookery book	☐ Storage tins
☐ Corkscrew	☐ Toaster
☐ Deep fat fryer	☐ Tumble drier
☐ Dishwasher	☐ Washing machine
☐ Food processor	☐ Wok
☐ Freezer	☐ Yoghurt maker
☐ Fridge	☐
☐ Iron and ironing board	☐
☐ Kettle	☐
☐ Knife set	☐

Style/Colour/Make   Style/Colour/Make

Personal items

Books

Calculator

Ornaments

Sports equipment

Style/Colour/Make

Miscellaneous

Style/Colour/Make

☐	Answering machine _____	☐	Umbrella stand _____
☐	Barbecue _____	☐	Vacuum cleaner _____
☐	Carpets _____	☐	Vases _____
☐	Clock _____	☐	Washing line _____
☐	Electric drill _____	☐	Wheelbarrow _____
☐	Garden fork _____	☐	Workmate bench _____
☐	Garden furniture _____	☐	Z-bed _____
☐	Garden spade _____	☐	_____
☐	Garden tools _____	☐	_____
☐	Hedge trimmer _____	☐	_____
☐	Ice bucket _____	☐	_____
☐	Lawn mower _____	☐	_____
☐	Linen basket _____	☐	_____
☐	Luggage _____	☐	_____
☐	Pictures _____	☐	_____
☐	Radio _____	☐	_____
☐	Rugs _____	☐	_____
☐	Stereo _____	☐	_____
☐	Telephone _____	☐	_____
☐	Tool box _____	☐	_____
☐	Tools _____	☐	_____
☐	Trays _____	☐	_____

Pre-Wedding Parties

Hen Party

Venue _____

Address _____

_____

Telephone _____

Date/time booked _____

Number of guests _____

Transport arrangements _____

Name	Address or Telephone	Invited	Reply (√ or ×)

Stag Party

Venue _____

Address _____

_____

Telephone _____

Date booked _____

Time _____

Number of guests _____

Transport arrangements _____

Name	Address or Telephone	Invited	Reply (√ or ✕)

Party for Family and Friends

Venue _____

Address _____

_____

Telephone _____

Date booked _____

Time _____

Number of guests _____

Transport arrangements _____

Name	Address or Telephone	Invited	Reply (√ or ✕)

The Honeymoon

First night destination _____

Address _____

_____

Telephone _____

Honeymoon destination _____

Hotel/villa/site address _____

_____

Telephone _____

Dates _____

Travel agent _____

Address _____

_____

Telephone _____

☐ Innoculations	☐ Washing things
☐ Passports	☐ Cosmetics
☐ Marriage certificate	☐ Contraception
☐ Visas	☐ Shampoo, hairdryer etc.
☐ Currency/travellers' cheques	☐ Jewellery
☐ Insurance	☐ Shoes
☐ Maps	☐ Coats
☐ Guidebooks	☐ Underwear
☐ Tickets	☐ Swimsuits
☐ Driving licences	☐ Nightclothes

☐ Car documents

☐ First aid kit

☐ Travel sickness tablets

☐

☐

☐

☐ Dressing gown

☐ Day clothes

☐ Evening clothes

☐

☐

☐

Luggage packed and loaded _____

Transport from reception _____

Departure time from reception _____

Airport/station _____

Departure time from airport/station _____

Flight/train number _____

Departure date for return journey _____

Departure time _____

Airport/station _____

Flight/train number _____

Transport home from airport/station _____

Changing your Name

Sample Letter

Dear Sir

I wish to inform you that following my marriage on 15 August 19—, I will be changing my name from Jane Mary Smith to Jane Mary Jones with immediate effect.

I would be grateful if you would make the necessary alterations to my bank account number 123456. Please inform me if you need any additional information, specimen signatures etc.

Yours faithfully

Remember to Inform

☐	Bank	☐	Insurance company
☐	Building society	☐	Mail order catalogues
☐	Clubs	☐	Passport office
☐	Credit card company	☐	Post Office (savings account)
☐	Department of Health	☐	Premium bonds
☐	Department of Social Security	☐	
☐	Dentist	☐	
☐	Doctor	☐	
☐	Driver and Vehicle Licensing Centre	☐	
☐	Employer	☐	
☐	Inland Revenue		

Index